CATALYST

The Moments that Change Everything

CW Allen

PUBLISHED BY

Catalyst

Published by the Dream Baby Creative
thecwallen.com
info@thecwallen.com
@thecwallen

Library of Congress Control Number: 2020907537

Paperback ISBN: 978-1-7346385-3-0
eBook ISBN: 978-1-7346385-4-7

Printed in the United States of America

Contents

Foreword

"I am, have been, and always will be a catalyst for change." These are the powerful words of Shirley Chisholm, congresswoman, civil rights leader, and the first African American woman elected to Congress and to run for the office of US President under a major party. Her story has been a catalyst in my life for pressing forward against insurmountable odds. On the campaign trail she often said she was excited to announce her candidacy for president despite the reality that the current climate of our country gave her no chance of actually gaining the office. When I read about her life, I often wonder what were her catalysts?

What causes a person to push forward even with little to no hope of change?

What is a catalyst? Why write a book with that as its focus? Often when we think of catalytic moments, we think of the outside forces that cause us to slightly change course, reconnect to previous ideals, or even rewrite an entirely new course of history. These indelible forces often initiate dreams that result in new goals, visions that become new plans, and even desires that become new realities.

How many of us actually take the time to think about the catalyst for change we hope to become? How many of us have taken the time to look back over the trajectory of our lives? Do we step back and see the unique and long lasting footprints left on us from our myriad of experiences and relationships? Have we paid attention to how they have molded us into the people we are today or hope to become in the future?

What intrigues many scholars about the life of Jesus Christ is not necessarily His religious language or acumen, the amazing miracles He performed, the number of followers He had, or the amazing words he said. It is the fact that centuries after His earthly ministry was complete, His lessons, life, and legacy still continue to linger. The lessons He taught are still being taught all over the world in sanctuaries and seminaries. The life He lived is still commemorated annually and dissected by scientists and scholars alike. The legacy He left has grown into the largest religion in the world and sparks equal amounts of controversy and hope. Without a doubt Jesus' life has truly become a catalyst in our current climate and culture.

When we peak behind the curtains of Jesus' life in the Bible we find the moments where He retreats from the busyness to reflect on His life. Moments where He reconnected to the Father, who He identifies as His catalyst. In the garden of Gethsemane we see Jesus being reminded, in the midst of a painful experience, that His purpose on the Earth was to do the will of the Father no matter the cost.

What CW Allen has done in this book is open himself up in a way that reminds us all of our need to live within this same balance. To reflect well in our lives and recognize the myriad of relational experiences that have been a catalyst in our lives, yet, with equal measure to hold ourselves accountable for how we can be a catalyst for change for our children, communities, cities, countries, and entire culture. I have had the tremendous privilege to walk alongside CW and his family for over a decade and to experience many of the moments that have made him the man he is today.

As you can imagine each of those moments were different. Some were painful and some were joyful. Some were expected and others caught him completely off guard. Regardless of what each moment has brought him, what I have seen consistently from CW is a commitment to his art, a passion for the city, a love for family, and a love for God that continues to inspire me.

In these pages is the heart and story of a man, who like Shirley Chisholm, *is, has been, and always will be a catalyst for change*. Through honest memoir, helpful anecdotes and healing messages, CW encourages us all to be a catalyst for change. Undoubtedly, his greatest mission in life is to point all who will listen to the One who has been his catalyst all along.

Jonathan "Pastah J" Brooks
Pastor, author, artist, and speaker

Prologue | Embracing The Catalyst

When Enoch had lived 65 years, he became the father of Methuselah. After he became the father of Methuselah, Enoch walked faithfully with God 300 years and had other sons and daughters. Altogether, Enoch lived a total of 365 years. Enoch walked faithfully with God; then he was no more, because God took him away.

—Genesis 5:21-24

Most of the time when I read the Bible, I skipped over the lineages but this particular one changed that. I realized that there is a story in family trees the authors share. It gives insight into the progression of their lives, communities, and even what God was doing during their generation. In Genesis 5 we see the same progression repeated for every person in the family tree until we get to Enoch, whose branch is slightly different.

As the author penned Enoch's line, he added that after he had Methuselah, Enoch walked with God for three hundred years and then God took him. I asked myself, why did the author decide to share that Enoch walked with God and not the others? What does it mean that he was taken by God? Why not just say he died like the others? As I processed this lineage to the narrative of the whole Bible, I came up with a simple answer. Enoch was so amazed and revived by his child's birth, that it change his life drastically.

One night I woke up to feed my two-week-old daughter and as I looked in her eyes, I had a similar experience. I prayed for her and asked God to help me be a great father. I prayed that she would be saved when she could understand our faith. I even thought about what songs would define our family memories. My drive to create was invigorated as I began writing this book and my next album. I even attempted to become a morning workout person. (That wasn't a good idea with a newborn.) I was burnt out from church culture, but I reaffirmed that an exodus from the local church was not an option for my family. She caused me to reevaluate every aspect of my life as she awakened me in joyful new ways.

People told me that I would love like I had never loved before. They told me I would miss her every moment we were apart. They said this would change me, and when she was born a switch would flip in my soul. I would daydream about having a family and being a father, and now that it's a reality, I am at a loss for words to express this gift, this catalyst. In scientific terms a catalyst is a substance that is introduced to another agent to elicit stimulation or a chemical change. People or things that precipitate an event are everyday catalysts. We all have experienced catalysts that have changed our life's trajectory from what we thought we knew to what God has in store for us.

Imagine God interjecting a great catalyst into our lives that makes us the people He created us to be. I will not lie to you. I am a dreamer, so the idea of creating excites me. I'm a seven on the enneagram personality test. The Enneagram consists of nine personality types. A seven is an enthusiast who's fixated on planning and anticipation, so the prospect of a new exciting moment gets me going. But I also struggle with abrupt changes, especially the ones that leave me with heartache. But, I'm learning that there is a marriage between beauty and brokenness. They are actually inseparable on this side of eternity. God doesn't allow us to be acquainted with true purpose apart from uncomfortable seasoning. So, I'm asking God to allow you and I to see our burdens and catalysts as opportunities to strengthen our character. The thought of embracing them still scares me to this day, but as I reflect on my short life, I'm reminded that God will be there every step of the way.

As you read my story, I pray that you are changed like Enoch. I'm trusting that your catalyst, rather good or bad, will produce a person that makes God and those watching well pleased.

Chapter 1 | Just A Kid From Cleveland

I was born on October 6, 1986 in the city of the 2016 world champion Cleveland Cavaliers. My dad told me when I was born, he had to name me CW after him. Naturally he thought about the people who teased him for his name and the countless times I would be asked what it stands for, yet nothing could derail him from giving me the gift of bearing his name.

Life in my early childhood was good. My father worked at various companies while my mother worked the swing shift at LTV Steel Company her whole career. My brother, Rob, and I loved our parents and rarely noticed that they were functioning drug addicts. My mom told me that she and dad got so high once on the way to Virginia for our family reunion that they circled the city for hours before returning home. Another time she took me with her to pick up drugs. I must have been four or five and out of nowhere I began yelling, "No, we shouldn't be here!" She was so creeped out she left. To this day I have no memory of that moment; it must have been God speaking through me.

When my mom and dad got divorced I was six years old, and I found myself spending a nice amount of time on E. Eighty-Seventh Street at Grand Honey's house. That's where Daddy moved to. Everyone on Eighty-Seventh was like family. I had lots of cousins who lived around the corner, and it seemed like every night everyone would come over for cookouts and card games. We spent countless hours playing basketball on cut-out crates we nailed to the street poles. Every time we put them up the cops would tear them down. Sometimes someone would bring a monkey wrench and crack open a fire hydrant for our hood water pad.

At the end of those days I hung with Daddy. He was always the go-to guy for a fun time filled with laughter. I remember the few times I went fishing with him and the long walks we took down Lake Shore Drive. I will never forget those summers.

During the week I lived with Grandma Cleo. Grandma Cleo was from Florida and had eight children. She and Grandpa Moss were married for decades before he passed away. While my mom was working and figuring out life, Grandma helped raise us. She taught me how to add and subtract, and we spent hours playing tic-tac-toe on the back of her *TV Guides* where she also wrote her numbers.

Since Grandma had adjusted to raising eight kids, she had her ways of doing things that were a little different than six-year-old Dub would have preferred. We never ate out or ordered pizza because Grandma cooked everything. Grandpa was a farmer who went south and brought back crops that would be stretched through the winter for their kids, so she continued the tradition of making all her food at home. There were also very little sweets in the house. Grandma was diabetic so the diet ginger ale was about as sweet as it got. Even though it was an adjustment I loved my grandma; she is such a special woman. Grandma Cleo is still living to this day at 102 years old.

My grandpa was a firm and loving man. I can still recall his voice and the times I spent exploring his basement workshop. I remember a peach tree and grape vine in his backyard that he had planted. Being a farmer from Georgia gave him a gift for cultivating just about anything you could think up. I've even heard rumors that he was a guitarist. When he passed away in 1992, it hit me hard; I wept for weeks.

Years later when I returned to visit my grandma, one of the neighbors asked me what I was up to. "I'm a youth minister," I told her. "I always knew you would be a preacher," she said. I was shocked. She told me my grandpa would sit me on his lap when I was little and read the Bible to me on the front porch. Soon after I would run up and down the street telling the kids they better be good, or they would go to hell. I may not be that rambunctious now, but it's wild to think my grandpa's small investment of time led to a reverence for God that countless people have benefitted from. God had been preparing me for years prior to my journey into the ministry.

Preteens

When I was ten years old my mother got clean and moved us to the west side. The west side was very different from the east side. There were lots of recreation centers, the kids didn't pick on us, and the people weren't all black. This was the first time I had lived in a neighborhood where there were as many white people as black ones. It was also the first time I encountered Puerto Rican people. I was so ignorant of any cultures outside of black and white that I assumed they were white as well.

My first west side friend was Junior. Jun, as everyone called him, was a little older, had a chip in his tooth, and was Puerto Rican. He had a large family that introduced us to Puerto Rican culture. I loved that it resembled ours but still was its own. They had a different language, parades, dope music, and were very tight knit. They found a way to create good times with very little, which always impressed me. I would be hypnotized in the summers because all the fine Puerto Rican girls came to the pool. They convinced me that Mama had finally made the right move.

By this time, I had officially hit me preteens and our family had grown, making me the oldest of four. This meant lots of responsibilities like watching after my siblings and still maintaining my example as the eldest child. I joined all the sports teams so that I could to get out of constant babysitting, though it never fully escaped me. Around that time is also when I met Jesus.

A friend of mine noticed I was reading a Bible at my desk and invited me to a club called Campus Life. At Campus Life they had video game systems, a three-on-three basketball tournament, snacks, and leaders who wanted to be in our lives. My first time going I raised my hand to receive Christ as my savior. I had already met Him earlier, but I needed to be sure that I really knew Him. I didn't want to go to hell if I got hit by a bus that night.

"Wait! You sound like you're saved already? Carl said.

"Yeah, I am. I just needed to get saved again because I stopped being saved after I sinned," I replied.

Carl Buzzard, Mike Harper, and Jeff Thompson sat with me at McDonalds that evening and explained to me that I didn't need to get saved again. I just needed to trust God and fight to be consistent. So, I did, and I began going to Scranton Road Bible Church with Mike's and Jeff's families. God really became real to me as I heard the messages from Pastor Joe, who would later become another father to me.

High School

It's been fifteen years, and I still remember high school like it was yesterday. I met my best friends the very first day of school, and we were inseparable. Diddy was nicknamed after the music mogul P. Daddy. Ejay was the guy who was gifted at everything he did. He could sing and girls loved that, plus he was a great athlete. Chad was Pastor Joe's son and a hooper with torch (good jump shot). Rodney rounded us out with his intellect and quiet strength.

We all played sports during the week and would often find ourselves at house parties and teen clubs making the most of my weekends. On Thursdays, when I would return to our church's youth group, it was like another person manifested himself. Sure, God was always in the back of my head as I exhausted my extrovert personality, but He rarely had the green light to take the driver's seat of my life.

During a cross-country practice, a friend from youth group came up to me and said, "CW, you're different here than you are at church."

She didn't accuse me of anything or call me a hypocrite. She just made an observation. But it was as if God used her observation to cut my heart in two. The next few days I internally wrestled with who I was. My best friends knew I was somewhat religious but never enough to impede my lifestyle. My church leaders allowed me to be a student leader, but they never realized the depth of my wretchedness. I was a mess and God was undoing me.

My junior year I stepped on campus determined to be who God made me to be. A friend of mine named Carlos looked at me and said, "When did you become so goddie!?" I took comments like that as a moral victory. If I was soliciting that type of attention for my faith, I knew I must have been doing something right.

Everyday A Rapper is Born

Later that year our youth group decided to throw an open mic event, and I was the MC (master of ceremonies). People didn't know it, but I was also secretly an emcee (rapper). I had a notebook full of poems and loose rap bars. While I was writing some on the school bus, my girlfriend alerted the whole bus that I was a rapper.

"He's been holding out! He about to have ya'll do stuff at the open mic, but he won't," she said.

"Dub drop some bars bruh!" one of the homies shouted out.

"Yeah, bro, let us hear something," another egged on.

I was terrified. I would rap at home for fun, but my art was for me and no one else. Sure, I was known for being an artist because I drew freehand, but this was different. It was Hip-Hop. Every day after school we crowded around Gio and whoever he was battling because we all loved and respected rap music. Seeing a rap battle was like watching a civilized beating. Hip-hop was our language. Those are the same people who were calling for me to spit some rhymes.

I cleared my throat and with hesitation began to rap. The back of the yellow bus was quiet, and I couldn't tell if they liked it since everyone was listening intently. When I finished the guy next to me slammed the back of his hand into my chest and extended his fingers to give me dap. I extended my hand in gratitude as my classmates showed me love for my hidden gift. Just like that I was locked in as a rapper.

Zeal for the King

After high school I consistently found myself at Christian open mics around the city. I had formed a rap group with my youth leaders Kyro Tylor and Aaron Buck. Our DJ, X, was a blind pianist who excelled in music production and recording. We spent hours in his closet recording into a pop filter we created with a hanger and stockings. There were a couple nights X and I started at 6 p.m. and realized we lost track of time as the sun rose twelve hours later. Those were pure and beautiful days early in my career.

I was excited and hungry to share God with my friends and family. I breathed the Bible and gospel rap. The last thing I needed to be official was a rap name, and I couldn't think of anything better to describe my personality than Zeal.

"Never be lacking in zeal, but keep your spiritual fervor, serving the Lord."

—Romans 12:11

Me and the guys not only continued rapping around the city, we also had a Bible study accountability group called the BruthaHood (BH). The BH forged some of my dearest friendships. Fifteen years later there's no way I would be an artist if it had not been for those men. I'm forever grateful for the moments we had in my journey.

The City Mission

In the summer following graduation I needed a job and was offered a position at the City Mission of Cleveland as a summer missionary working with kids. The City Mission not only had programs for kids, it also housed a nationally renowned men's shelter and clothing drive. Lots of the high school seniors I counseled that year were the same age as me. I had to be as mature as I possibly could so they wouldn't pull my card. By the end of the summer they were shocked that Mr. CW was actually their age.

We spent weeks away working the mission's camp grounds with Elder Lynda, Ms. Cass, and Luvirt. Each week was a different age group and tone. Elder Lynda led the middle and high school groups with sensitivity to God's spirit. She challenged me to be in tune to God's miraculous work. I appreciate how she taught me to be perceptive to God's voice. Ms. Cass was an artist. She specialized in using music and creativity to teach the elementary-aged children. She taught me how to nurture the children I ministered to. Luvirt was a theologian who loved Christian rap. Every day he would stop me in the halls and recite his favorite Cross Movement lyrics. He demonstrated a consistent firm character that we all admired.

The two years I worked for the mission I wrestled with idea of going into full-time ministry. It was obvious I was gifted for it and I really loved God, but I was afraid of what it would mean for my life. A lot of the ministers I knew raised money to work. I had no desire to beg for money since I grew up in poverty. They also lived a life that was so opposite from what I saw every day. I honestly didn't know if I fit the mode of what I thought a minister should look like.

It didn't take long for me to become resigned to the fact that I should just be on the radio or something while doing ministry on the side. Fortunately, God wouldn't let up as He kept showing and affirming me in ministry. I kept getting more and more opportunities where I just couldn't deny it anymore. I soon enrolled in evening Bible classes at the City Mission through Moody Bible Institute.

I was confronted with the richness of God's word as Pastor Warren Maddox taught me hermeneutics (how to study the Bible) and Bible observation skills. Pastor Maddox also taught me that I needed to love God with my mind as well as my emotions. God didn't just want me to cry for Him. He also wanted me to think deeply about Him. One day doctor Maddox was furious with me because I turned in an untyped half done paper.

"CW! What is this? You're taking this class for credit. You need to take this seriously. God wants to use you, but you have to be serious. Stop bullshitting the text!"

Needless to say, I straightened up and left his class with a B.

My hunger to know more about God only intensified, which led me to leave home and go off to Bible college. Anyone who knows me will tell you that I love Cleveland. I love the underdog mentality it has ingrained in me. I love the many summer memories and the diverse melting pot of people. If you would have told me I was going to leave my beloved "mistake on the lake" I would have told you that you're a false prophet. But sure enough the call was clear, and I was on my way to Bible college.

Chapter 2 | He Over Does it

God met me as I sat in the packed Atlanta auditorium. There were two thousand black college students assembled for the Impact Movement's National Conference. The conference was filled with dynamic black Christian thought leaders from all over the country: Priscilla Shirer, James White, Da T.r.u.t.h., Lecrae, Eric Mason, Israel Houghton, Kirk Franklin, and The Ambassador. It still gives me chills thinking about what we got while we were there.

Christian Hip-Hop artist The Ambassador shouted: "God doesn't just do it! He overdoes it!" As he shared about God taking the small things and people of the Bible to do amazing works, I was inspired to trust God more, to believe that my life was a part of those small things He wanted to use.

Going to College

When I went to visit Moody Bible Institute, I knew it was the place where I wanted to pursue my biblical education. My pastor, Joe Abraham, and the pastor before him both attended Moody, and if it could help me become half the teacher that Pastor Joe was, I was all-in. The campus was tucked in the center of downtown Chicago, so I would have access to all my needs. The Chi, as it has been affectionately called, was appealing to me. It was big and beautiful.

During our campus tour I found out that the prestigious institution accepted only 20 percent of applicants. I didn't know if I would make the cut, but I knew that I loved what they were about, and I decided I couldn't let what ifs get in the way. I applied in April and was told I would hear if I was accepted by October. As the months passed, I anxiously awaited but never heard anything. One afternoon I was awakened from a nap by a call from an admissions counselor at Moody named Donnie.

"Hey, Bro, you coming to The Chi?" she said enthusiastically.

"Hey, Donnie, I don't think I got in. They never reached out to me," I replied.

"Wait, what! You should have heard something even if you didn't get in! Let me check on this."

After we hung up Donnie did some digging and found out that my application was misplaced in the previous semesters' files and had never been reviewed. She got a committee together to see if they would accept me on the spot. After months of waiting and praying, I was finally accepted and officially heading to Chicago.

Unfortunately, my excitement was squelched when I realized that Moody didn't have an in-house loan program. They also didn't accept federal application for student aid (FASA). They were a private Christian school, and in order to not jeopardize their work, they chose not to accept government funding. Moody gave students free tuition, but you still had to pay for books, school fees, and room and board. These fees totaled about five thousand dollars a semester. For a student coming from the hood this was a daunting amount. I couldn't ask my mom to help because she had my three siblings to raise, and I didn't have five grand lying in the bank. I was truly depending on God's grace to make a way.

My mom and I went to multiple banks to inquire about private loans, but the interest rates were crazy and unhealthy for our family. They also would require me to begin making payments following the semester of disbursement. That meant I'd have to begin paying back the loan while I was still going to school full time. I couldn't imagine paying large loans and doing school with no prospects of a job. Needless to say, I began to believe God was truly closing the door for me to attend Moody. What if I had been putting all my eggs in the wrong basket? What if God wanted me to look into another Bible college?

I decided It was best to pursue other options. I applied to Lancaster Bible College (LBC), the college of my Christian Hip-Hop hero the Ambassador. They accepted FASA and had an in-house loan program. I had spent plenty of years visiting Philly for Christian Hip-Hop concerts and conferences, so I developed a healthy respect for its east coast culture. Also my homie Michael Blue was attending there that semester. It all seemed perfect, but God still wouldn't let me put my Moody acceptance away. It kept coming up in conversations. I thought I had moved on, but I kept finding myself wondering could I find a way to make it work.

To this day I am still blown away by how my home church in Cleveland loved me since I walked through their doors as a scrawny pre-teen. The scholarship committee offered me two thousand dollars to attend school but was concerned I might not be able to figure out the rest. Still I felt like God wanted me at Moody, so I decided not attend Lancaster even though the package seemed perfect.

As they say, "If it's God's will it's his bill." That's how I got through school and a decade of ministry. God used people, many of whom I least expected to meet my needs. On my last weekend in Cleveland a sister from church came up to me and said, "I believe in you and I'm investing in you" as she put money in my hand. Another caught me on the way out the door and handed me two dollars to go to school. I knew her gift was sacrificial, and I also knew that God was using her to say I will provide for you no matter where I call you to go.

I worked as many hours as the campus would allow. All my checks went to paying my tuition. When I wasn't working, I was learning all of studies of the Bible: soteriology, pneumatology, eschatology, ecclesiology. Often, I found my financial efforts weren't enough and when I thought my journey at Moody was ending an anonymous gift would appear on my tuition bill. One time a doctor heard my need and sent two thousand dollars. Another time I found a forty dollar check and a sweet note from my good friend back home in my mailbox. Little did she know I just ran out of deodorant and basic toiletries, so her gift was right on time. This was my life during my time at Moody, and in a small way I learned what the Apostle Paul meant when he said:

> I am not saying this because I am in need, for I have learned to be content whatever the circumstances. I know what it is to be in need, and I know what it is to have plenty. I have learned the secret of being content in any and every situation, whether well fed or hungry, whether living in plenty or in want. I can do all this through him who gives me strength. (Philippians 4:11-13)

Sunshine Gospel Ministries

With my spring semester ending I needed to find a job to pay for fall. My friend Brian Dye told me about a small ministry on the South Side looking for summer youth ministry workers. The job seemed perfect for me because I had worked with youth in a similar context the past few years in Cleveland. As I approached Sunshine Gospel Ministries it weirdly felt like home. The Woodlawn neighborhood where it is located is similar to the neighborhoods both my grandmas lived in back home and the staff members were very family oriented.

Soon after being hired Sarah Avery became my spades partner at most cookouts. She is a very compassionate person who adopted random animals and would fight any system for you. Dave Clark was my roommate and mentor. He is a stocky white guy who many compared to the Chicago Bears great Brian Urlacher. His sense of humor reminds me of a character from the office, and his jokes would set the room on fire. Pete was his right-hand man and affectionately known as Pastor Pete. He is stoic and at first I wondered if he liked me, but as I got to know him and his family, they became some of my closest friends. Then there was Brittney the craft master. She was my partner in youth work. These were the folks I spent most of my time with during my first two years in Chicago.

During our first orientation the tenured staff walked us through the dynamics of our neighborhood. I was shocked to see all the correlations to the gospel, black history, and social justice. As our executive director, Joel, began to talk through the details of biblical shalom (peace), it was as if another dimension of my faith was unlocked. I knew God saved us from sin and was making us more like him, but Joel explained to us that God is making all things new.

I had always thought we just needed to convert people before He came back and burnt everything up. I thought He was going to make a new heaven and Earth from scratch and completely throw the old ones away. I always thought focusing on justice too much was getting away from what God called us to do: be holy. But Joel's deeper, wholistic look at Scripture provided me countless examples of

God being a great steward who was making all things as they were intended to be. He was making right the wrongs of people and the groaning creation. In other words, this world is not just a burning ship from which people need to escape. It is our home that needs to be redeemed. Internalizing this helped me to understand my purpose in this age as I anticipate the next one.

Do not conform to the pattern of this world [temporary age or time period], but be transformed by the renewing of your mind. Then you will be able to test and approve what God's will is—his good, pleasing and perfect will.

—Romans 12:2

I'm struck by how often we only think about the virtuous traits of being a believer but not the tangible call of meeting physicals needs. If we fight for lives in the womb, we should use the same energy to support the lives outside of it. If we are voting, we should think of our neighbors (the least of these) more than our own interest. If we value comfort over compassion, we have missed God's mark. But if we really think about God's will on earth as it is in heaven, we will be compelled to be *humble, merciful,* and *just* people. I never imagined starting a summer internship that would add to my faith so much, but God never ceases to provide. He doesn't just do it; He overdoes it!

Chapter 3 | Facing My Demons

As I looked at the back of the room I was determined not to cry. Even though it was one of the few moments where tears were justified, I was not having it. Then she happened. The most beautiful woman in the world walked through the back doors of the church. She was so elegant. I couldn't contain myself as everyone rose to their feet and she waltzed down the aisle. I couldn't believe I was going to marry her. I never imagined I would come to Chicago and meet my wife! As I finished rapping my vows, I had no doubt I just made one of the best decisions of my life.

I had been dating my wife for two and a half years prior to our marriage, and it was such a unique experience for me. I had had other relationships, but this relationship with my wife changed my whole being. It made me question if I really trusted God with my romantic life, and if I was really a man worthy of being a husband.

I remember when my mama met her, and she was extremely impressed. She said, "Ok Dub, you only get three. If you mess this one up you gone miss out."

We both laughed, but deep inside I was praying that I wouldn't mess this one up. To fully unpack why I felt this way, I need to take you back to my childhood.

My First Kiss

My brother Rob and I would spend hours playing outside on our big wheels and catching bugs in the summer. One cloudy summer day we were playing with our next-door neighbor Jessica. Jessica lived with her grandparents only in the summer, so it was always a special treat to see her.

During that time Nintendo was becoming popular and every kid wanted a Gameboy. Our parents didn't buy us stuff like that but Jessica's did, and she had a Gameboy. I would dream about playing it. She offered to let me play it in exchange for a kiss. The idea of kissing a girl was so gross, but I was desperate for that Nintendo action, so I went along with it. I didn't think too deeply about it, but eventually one kiss became day in and day out of slob sessions. I just imitated what I had seen the people in my grandma's soap operas do. Eventually I had forgotten all about the Gameboy, and my little brother downstairs on the steps playing it. Kissing became fun.

Curious

I wasn't totally sure why we were moving with my Grandma Cleo when we had our own house, but

I just listened to Mama and didn't question it. My mother and father were officially separated, and I hated it. Sure, my father wasn't super attentive to us at times, and he drank a lot, but I loved him; he was my hero. But my mother just couldn't take it anymore, and she decided she needed a change.

My brother and I spent a lot of time with my grandma and my mean old Uncle John. Since Grandma was older and couldn't entertain us, we found ourselves spending hours exploring the house and creating superhero adventures. While exploring one of the closets, I accidentally hit a wall and knocked a small black bag from the top shelf. I was sure I hit the jackpot and found some candy or something. I unzipped the bag and found a bunch of tapes, many of which had "xxx" on them. I remember my mother telling me I wasn't allowed to watch stuff that had "xxx" on it. I was curious to see why, so I popped one in the VCR. I didn't know what to make of what I was seeing. Were they wrestling? The kissing on these movies wasn't like me and Jessica's. It was something different. I couldn't stop watching. Over the next months I spent hours watching them, and just like that I was a seven-year-old porn addict.

I Didn't See That One Coming

My hormones were raging as I was stepping into my preteens. Watching pornography was not satisfying my appetite anymore. I was sure I was ready for sex. So that summer I was determined to get some. As the summer approached my plans took a turn I didn't expect. I got the opportunity to spend the summer with my Uncle Al's family in Michigan. Going to Michigan was so exciting because we never went out of town; all I knew was Cleveland. I had two older cousins who I looked up too. One of them had a son a couple years younger than me, so I had a homie to kick it with most days.

One night we were playing Mortal Kombat with my older cousin Lil Al. After beating me he began to do a fatality (the final move in the fighting round of Mortal Kombat) on me. The screen showed a scene where the character turned into a skeleton and blew fire everywhere. For some reason that prompted me to ask my cousin about hell and rumors of the world coming to an end in 2000.

"Al do you think the world is coming to an end in 2000?" I asked.

I was sure he would say no, but to my surprise he said he did. Al was studying to be a minister and knew a lot about God, so my mind went into a whirlwind. It was 1999; I was only eleven years old, which meant I would be twelve when I died! I wanted to grow up, have a family, and of course . . . have sex.

"What am I gonna do?!" I exclaimed.

"Do you know Jesus?" He replied.

"Everybody knows Jesus, Al." I answered with confidence.

"No, not know *about* God, Dub. Do you know God?"

At that point I was confused. Then he began to explain the difference between knowing God and knowing about God. It was as clear as day. I knew that If the world ended in 2000, I was not going to be with God because I didn't know him for real.

"What do I do Al? How do I know Him?"

My cousin then proceeded to pray with me, and I asked God to save me from my sins and accept me as his child. I didn't know anything about Him except what I saw on the occasional Easter Sunday when we attended church. I Didn't know what to expect, but I was glad to know Jesus. When I did wrong, I felt a heavier regret. Something was different, and I couldn't explain it.

One time I was watching TV with Al, and I began to explain how I would give it (sex) to a fine woman I saw on TV. Then he explained that having sex out of marriage was a sin. I didn't know what to do with that information. I still planned on trying to get some when I got back home. Why would something that looked so good be sin? That's where the reality that this new faith thing was about to be the hardest decision I had ever committed to. How could I love Jesus and keep watching my xxx videos? Would He understand if I did it one time before the world ended? Sure enough life was about to change, and I didn't see this one coming.

Back Like I Never Left

When I returned home I was excited about my new faith. My cousin had spent hours teaching me about God, and I had made up my mind that I would be a serious Christian. I was slaying all my friends in the spirit and getting teased by the local dope boys for proclaiming I wanted to become a reverend. As my first semester of middle school approached, my new faith was weaning. By the time I left Lincoln Junior my rollercoaster high had ended, and it was off to a new high.

I didn't realize it then, but I was a very oversexualized tween. I would tell lots of dirty jokes and make countless passes at the girls around me. I was a relatively good kid, but I just didn't know what to do with my hemi-powered sex drive. I was conflicted as I attempted to balance my porn and newfound masturbation addiction with my Campus Life Christian activities. It only got worse my first summer out of high school because that's when I lost my virginity. Initially I was very excited and loved it, but then my conviction sent me crashing down. I repeated this cycle a few times.

My senior year I felt like I had experienced some victory in the area of my purity because I had only been making out and stopped having sex my sophomore year. I became an advocate for the True Love Waits movement in our region. A newspaper even wrote a piece about me and my commitment. A few youth groups asked me to come and share about living pure. I was happy to do anything to help others grow in their faith and receive positive affirmation from my leaders. The affirmation actually filled the void I had been missing from putting down porn and sex. It made me feel like I mattered.

My junior year I met a young lady who stole my heart. She was very beautiful and fun to be around. Our friendship quickly progressed. It was really innocent at first but then we found ourselves kissing and becoming more intimate. I remember making out with her one night and then preaching about purity the next. I hated myself in that moment. As I preached and looked out at her I felt like such a hypocrite. I hated that I would have months of honoring God with my purity, and I failed so miserably other times.

Am I Ready?

As time went on, I was rapping and speaking all over Ohio. I just could not *not* tell people about God's love for them. It was clear to me that even in my failures God set me apart to do ministry, but I was reluctant. I would give every excuse in the book as to why I wasn't qualified to serve God. (Sometimes I still do.) Fortunately for me, God saw something in me that I couldn't see in myself.

Before I left to Bible college I remember my pastor saying I was going to go away and find my wife. Part of me wanted to believe that, but I had just come out of a couple tough relationships that really made me examine myself. I had gotten to the point where I was afraid I'd be hurt again. I just couldn't handle another blow, so I dismissed it.

My sophomore year of college all that went out the window when I met Jacqueline "Jacqui" White. Jacqui was gorgeous and really loved God. She was really different, though. Jacqui was very devout and had never had a boyfriend before. She hadn't even kissed a boy. When she told me that she wanted to wait till she was married to even kiss a man, I was intrigued. I had been pure for a couple years, and shortly before I met Jacqui I had been consistently asking God to please send me a wife. I wondered if she could be the woman I had been praying about.

I asked Jacqui out on a date. She awkwardly resisted at first, but after a few jokes, she could tell I wasn't a creep and said yes. After a few months I knew she was wifey material, but I didn't know if she believed I was husband material. I told her bits about my past and lots of it made her uncomfortable. She had envisioned a husband who would give his first everything to her as she was to him, but I couldn't give her that. It caused lots of tension our first year. She drove me to my knees more than anything ever had. I began to want to fight for her. In the past I had no problem ending a relationship but not this time. The thought of losing her made me sick to my stomach. I realized I was in love. I realized I wanted to marry her.

This relationship changed my life in so many ways. God gave me a love for Jacqui that empowered me to protect her purity. When we reached two years I asked her to marry me. Even though I have a checkered past, my wife trusts me because she knows I sacrificed my own desires to honor her. It meant the world to me to be able to look at her father and say I kept my word and honored his daughter.

I'm so thankful for Jacqui because she is a visible example of God's grace to me. She accepted me when I struggled to accept myself. Her intelligence and humility have taught me to love others better.

I hope this chapter encourages you regardless of where you are in your relationship journey. I opened the door to sex too early, and it awakened something I wasn't able to tame. I know that every day of my life will be a fight. I believe if we fight to love God, He is willing to gift us with his grace until we are finally free no matter how much we fall. I feel like the Apostle Paul when he said

---

"This is a faithful saying, and worthy of all acceptation, that Christ Jesus came into the world to save sinners; of whom I am chief." (1 Tim 1:15)

Chapter 4 | Elephants and Stallions

As I sat on the ground with my arms wrapped around my knees, I couldn't believe I was actually crying. I wasn't just crying I was sobbing like a child who lost his snack. The last time I cried like that was ten years earlier when my grandma died. I was struck by what had just happened to me; I wasn't ready for it one bit.

The Crucible

Things had been going great. Like in Cleveland my musical and speaking presence began to pick up in Chicago. I was happily married a few years and ready to experience all the things I had spent my early twenties preparing for. I was excited about life and ready for God to show up and show out.

My DJ, Ruckus, and I had just finished a show in downtown Chicago, and I noticed he seemed lighter than usual (at least emotionally cause there's nothing light about Ruckus). As we began to talk, he shared with me about a life-changing trip he had been on called the Crucible.

"You mean like a Promise Keepers conference?" I asked.

"No not at all."

"Then what was it; what happened there?"

"I can't tell you. You just got to go, he said with wide eyes.

"Bro, I ain't with that cult stuff," I said. "You need to tell me something if you trying to get me to this joint. How much is it?"

"It's four hundred dollars, Bro, but it's worth every dime."

In my mind that settled it. There was no way I was spending four hundred dollars on a spooky mystery trip. For weeks he petitioned with me...

"Bro, you have to go! Don't miss out! I'll pay a portion of it for you."

I had been to "life-changing" Christian stuff during the previous two years and left more broke and frustrated than when I got there. Surely this trip wouldn't be any different. Every Crucible weekend trip that came up I passed on, but Ruckus kept inviting me to the next one. Over the next several months men I respected from all over Chicago began to talk about the mysterious life-changing experience. After being invited by ten or so men, I was convinced either they thought I was really jacked up or they were so compelled by the results of the trip that they couldn't help but refer as many men as possible.

Finally, Pastor Phil Jackson, pastor of the House Hip-Hop Covenant Church, cornered me. I didn't have any excuses in my calendar to bale me out of going. I couldn't use money because he got me a scholarship that covered all but the hundred-dollar deposit, and he even arranged a ride for me. With much hesitation I halted my busy life and committed to attend.

Tried by The Fire

As we entered the semi-lit campground, we were given strict instructions not to talk. The first man who talked to me was the camp leader who asked me a simple question:

"What do you want?"

I looked at him with a puzzled expression. He sternly asked, "Why are you here?"

The months leading up to the Crucible I was really wrestling with my job and feeling extremely burnt out. The weight of my community's angst was more real to me than ever. My passion for music intensified, but I knew there was no way to fully lean into my craft. My soul just needed a second wind from God. As I arrived at the Crucible, I already knew I just wanted to see or hear from God. I wasn't sure what that meant, but I was open to it.

With full vulnerability I told the camp leader: "I'm looking for direction. I'm wondering what God wants me to do next with my life."

His piercing blue eyes bore into my soul. That moment felt like hours. He looked at me like a child who disobeyed his parent, and I wondered if I said something wrong. Was he about to say I wasn't ready or worthy enough for this mysterious experience? He pointed to his left and said, "See the next man."

The next man made me choose an animal that represents my current place in life. After some prayer and thought, I chose an elephant.

Elephants are extremely powerful, but they can also be extremely timid. When a circus elephant is being trained, it is chained to a peg that is nailed into the ground. The baby elephant then musters its strength and attempts to run forward, it soon learns that the limitations of its confinement are too great to conqueror. As It becomes an adult, it remembers that single experience and never defies the limitations of the small peg again. I felt that my dreams and gifts were like the power and strength of the elephant. For some reason I couldn't will myself to be bold and rip the peg in the ground holding me at bay.

The last night of my time at the Crucible is when the real work began. I watched man after man ball up in tears as they confronted their struggles and strongholds. As the camp leader confronted me again, I began to process why I was like the fearful elephant. I was young with an extremely supportive wife, no health issues, no student debt, no children, or major obligations, so what was holding me back from stepping into being the artist God wired me to be. I had always been known as a person of great faith, so why was I so fearful in this particular area?

I wrestled with these questions for a solid hour and realized it all came back to my father. My daddy made sure that I knew he loved me. He gave me goofy nicknames that twisted the syllables of our shared name. He played with me and hugged me often. I never doubted that I was his little Dub. When he got drunk, he became a preacher and was one of the most motivating people you'll ever meet (lol).

"You're my Dub, and you can do anything!" he'd say.

I believed him with all my heart when he would say that. The problem was, I never saw him believe that for himself. So I internalized what I saw in him, and I never really believed I could do these great things with my life because my daddy never did them with his. His drinking and depression stunted his purpose and surely something would stunt mine if I tried too.

After my time of sobbing and feeling the weight of my father's pain, I began to deal with my own complacency. I could no longer allow this weight to hold me down. When my moment of being tried in the Crucible fire had ended, Pastor Phil asked me a question I will never forget.

"Elephant, what is you new name?"

Without any thought I chose Black Stallion. Stallions are graceful, intelligent, and powerful. They also possess another quality that I strive to have as a man. They are meek. The world around us sees the word *meek* as being weak, but that's not how it's used in the Bible. A weak person can't do what they desire, but meek people can do whatever they want yet they choose not to. To be meek is to have your power under control. Jesus was meek. He knew exactly when to put His godliness on full display and when to hold back.

Jesus' brothers said to Him, "Leave Galilee and go to Judea, so that your disciples there may see the works You are doing. No one who wants to become a public figure acts in secret. Since you are doing these things, show yourself to the world"

(John 7:3-5). For even His own brothers did not believe in Him.

"My time has not yet fully come" (John

7:-7-8)

Therefore, Jesus told them, *"my time has not yet here. The world cannot hate you, but it hates me, because I testify that its works are evil. You go to the festival. I am not going up to this festival, because my time has not yet fully come"* (John 7:-7-8).

Jesus understood that He was powerful, but He wasn't impressed with shallow validation. His meekness was an example to us all. I came to the Crucible as a searching elephant and left to begin my journey as a meek black stallion.

Chapter 5 | Stepping Off the Boat

D ub, you just got to do it man. It's time to step off the boat."

"Your wife is on board, no kids, and you're good at making music. What you are waiting on?"

"You only have a small window while your music is relevant. Don't miss that. The church has always struggled with fully embracing artists and their gifts. Don't let that get in the way."

These are all wise words I soaked up as I talked with my longtime friend, and mentor, Pastor Jon Brooks(Pastah Jay). Even though I had tremendous growth during the Crucible weekend It was still a process in getting to where I needed to be. I sat with Jay conflicted about stepping away from my comfortable job in youth ministry to chart the unknown seas of full-time artistry.

When I left Cleveland to attend Bible college, I did so knowing I could study the Bible and communications. Studying communications allowed me to grow in various concentrations surrounding music. Biblical studies trained me to rightly divide God's word. It was an amazing experience, but during my first few years in the Chi, God threw me a curveball called Young Life(An International Youth organization). At Sunshine Gospel Ministries we began a partnership with Young Life that allowed me to participate in doing full-time youth work.

Sunshine and youth ministry seemed like the perfect fit for me. I eventually settled in and became excited about the possibility of being planted there the next twenty or so years. Around my sixth year I started to struggle to do my job in an undivided way. I felt disillusioned at having passed up on touring opportunities. While I was working hard giving it my all, I lacked over-the-top ambition and dedication. If you've ever had an enthusiastic youth leader, you know what I'm talking about—that extra little bit that made them rush to the local school and fill out stacks of volunteer paperwork and become a coach. Or the will to spend sleepless nights dreaming of the next youth outing.

I constantly asked myself what it would look like to carve out a living doing the things I'm most passionate about. What if I were able to create jobs or scholarship dollars for others through my music? How great would it be to build God's kingdom by writing well-polished albums, books, and curriculums for inner city ministries! How amazing would it be for kids growing up like I did to encounter God through Jesus-loving Hip-Hop artists like I did? But these were just pipe dreams because I was too divided to capitalize on them.

But Jesus immediately said to them: "Take courage! It is I. Don't be afraid." "Lord, if it's you," Peter replied, "tell me to come to you on the water." "Come," he said. Then Peter got down out of the boat, walked on the water and came toward Jesus. But when he saw the wind, he was afraid and, beginning to sink, cried out, "Lord, save me!" Immediately Jesus reached out his hand and caught him. "You of little faith," he said, "why did you doubt?" (Matthew 14:27-31)

Like Peter, I found myself wondering if I could step off the boat and do something I had never dreamed of doing. Was I good enough to survive the winds and waves of life that could take my eye off what God had shown me to be true? If I sank, would the Lord catch me before I drowned?

The following months God sent countless reminders that He was in control of my fears. One afternoon a former worker of Sunshine came to visit. I had heard of her before, but we had never formally met. After giving her a tour of the facility, she asked me what God was doing in my life. I didn't know if she was ready for my spill, but for some reason I felt comfortable enough to begin vomiting my tensions. It could have only been God at work because she challenged me to be bold and do what was obvious.

Before I go any further you have to know that I am a risk taker, but a calculated one. I am very cautious with huge life changes. I never planned on leaving Cleveland, EVER. I waited two years before I proposed to my wife whom I fell in love with our first month of dating. I agonize over songs I put out, and I am a firm believer in long-term faithfulness. Unlike many of my millennial peers, I love the comfort and consistency of staying put. Naturally, I wrestled with leaving my first career of seven years.

For most of my time in ministry I raised monthly support as a missionary, so to me that was the most seamless way to support myself during the transition. That week I googled ministries for artists and found a small nonprofit that focused on sending artistic missionaries called Artist in Christian Testimony International (A.C.T. Intl). When I called, Judie the receptionist made me feel at home. One week later I was accepted as a member. The following months were fresh and exciting for me as I watched pieces of the puzzle come together. It's crazy how sometimes we create fears and narratives that God never intended for us to have.

Black Boy Rapping

My first year as a full-time artist I began booking shows in the fall for my spring and summer seasons. I was excited to share my new music because I knew it was riddled with faith, hope, and love that would encourage my listeners. As I began calling a large list of ministries and organizations in the Midwest, I became discouraged around the twentieth call. I got tired of hearing "oh, we don't allow rap here" or "that's not for us." I'm talking about churches in cities! Pastah Jay was right on the money when he said:

> Not only has the church forsaken individuals but often entire cultures. One culture that the church has done a poor job of connecting with is Hip-Hop. Even in this age of multiculturalism and ethnically diverse worship practices, Hip-Hop music and culture are still considered a novelty.

One promoter of a festival emailed me five months later and said thanks for reaching out to us, we really enjoyed having you in the past, but we have decided to only do a contemporary Christian music (CCM) stage at our festival this year. I was perplexed that a Christian organization in the middle of a non-Christian festival wouldn't include the world's most popular musical genre to attract their listeners. "You mean to tell me you're only going to do predominately white CCM in 2018, and you're trying to reach a generation of people infused with Hip-Hop culture?" I wondered.

Shortly after that I began to listen to interviews from other black Christian artists who didn't run in evangelical church circles with their music anymore. One particular interview really caught my attention as I listened intently to Hip-Hop artist Thi'sl share his story:

> "One of the most discouraging things in me doing CHH (Christian Hip-Hop) is that I knew that I wouldn't have as many opportunities because I'm hood and I make black hood music. If I made music that sound CCM I would be cool."

While interviewing in Orlando (one of the largest CHH markets and one of his best markets), Thi'sl was asked to share a live acapella performance of a song. When he finished, the whole station loved it. People were singing the words with him and everything. The owner of the station happened to be there and asked if that was a new song. Thi'sl explained that it wasn't new, and he sent it to the owner a year prior. The owner remembered receiving the song and assured Thi'sl he would go back and check it out.

With enthusiasm Thi'sl listened to that station during his whole trip in Orlando, but he never heard his song play on the air waves. He was shocked since his fans in that community were asking for it, and a lot of songs on the station sounded like his. Thi'sl decided he needed to call the owner to ask personally why they wouldn't play his record. The owner answered very honestly and said our board said your music sounds too ghetto. Then after talking about other artists on the station who had darker messaging in their Hip-Hop music but were white, the owner said "Thi'sl let's be honest, we're trying to reach white people."

After that call he sobbed as he told a friend, "The people who are supposed to be supporting me won't support me because I'm black. It crushed me."

As I continued my booking journey, I googled Christian festivals in the United States, and I found a site for all the year's events. My soul was grieved as I noticed that every one of them had a predominately white CCM or rock lineup of artists and speakers. There would be one or so Hip-Hop artists, and a lot of the time the Hip-Hop artists were white as well. What do I do with that as a black Christian artist who does Hip-Hop? Where do we belong? This was just one reminder that I wasn't home.

That same year I called my friend to ask If he could help in getting me a spot at a conference prominently for urban Christian folks. I loved (and still do) this conference. I had performed at it in the past but never pressed the issue of sharing again. I figured I would wait for a moment when the many leaders I knew there, would welcome me back as a minister. Every year following my performance I would go as an attendee or volunteer, and folks kept asking me if I was going to perform again. Six years had passed since my last performance, so I followed the prompting of the dozen or so folks and asked to come back and share.

I didn't have high expectations, but I figured I could get a small set somewhere in the festivities or maybe even teach a seminar of something. I noticed that there had been people with similar numbers in their social following (or less than mine) in the previous years, so I figured I was in a good spot to ask. Others with similar education and ministry experience were also invited, so I figured why not me.

I was told that their spots for Hip-Hop artists would be decreased to about a dozen artists that year, and that I could apply to compete for a spot at a showcase. I had applied for the showcase three years straight and felt discouraged with the process, so I passed on it. I had grown in my craft over the years since my last performance and I'd been faithful in ministry, so I just assumed that my good friend would affirm that with an opportunity somehow.

He was great about it but also honest about me not having whatever it took to warrant a spot. I wasn't mad, but after some hours of reflecting I was extremely discouraged. He didn't say I wasn't a strong enough performer, or he didn't value my gifts. He wasn't condescending, and he didn't say I wasn't a mature enough Christian to rock with them. But that's what I began to internalize about myself. I became more disappointed that I wasn't good enough for another Christian circle.

Pivot

I began to take some time to plan out my goals and vision for the next year. As I did so my philosophy became clear. I didn't want to chase being a "Christian celebrity." I wanted to genuinely meet people where they are. I didn't want to fight my way into the politics of evangelicalism and Christian music culture, so I simplified everything.

I began writing lyrics that incorporated themes of my faith but rarely called for straightforward repentance. I began to foster conversations with everyone. My church bookings went down, but my shows at smaller mainstream events increased. I became a regular at Christian camps and colleges that desired to encourage their youth and young adults who wrestled with or lacked a Christian identity. I loved encouraging people who were hurting. They often say things like:

"Nigga that $%*t was raw."

"I f%$K with the God thing you doing."

"You like a young Christian Kanye."

"Thank you for being so bold about your faith in a place like this. I am the only Christian in my band and that encouraged me."

I wouldn't say I am divorced from the idea of making music exclusively in the church context, but I step with caution these days. I just find it invigorating being an artist for the people with no barriers.

I Love Christian rap, and all that it's been

But if I'm honest ain't been feeling when I'm listening in

A lot of the music is feeling trite, adulting is getting light

Whoever fly the highest is jacking another's flight

I accepted the call, but the politics played

If I'm lacking co-sign records won't get played

If the music ain't fluffy then I won't get booked

And circles seem small when ya hue look cooked

Peter Pan, I know that my shadow coming

Elm street dreams I hear the claws strumming

Only so long before you figure ya niche

I gave my twenty's to the motions now I'm making a switch

So, You can keep ya boxes, I'm boxing out of it

Jumping over it, homie I'm cross fit

Unsaid Things | Catalyst Album

Chapter 6 | Roses

I never look down on ya, nothing but pride.

Rap with my real name to keep your pretense alive.

People don't get the flowers while they can enjoy the scent.

So, here's my bouquet, I just needed to vent.

— Vent | CW Allen Album

I've always been protective of my father. For some reason he's always had a special place in my heart. Maybe it's because when I was born he looked at my mom and said this is my little Dub, and named me CW Allen Jr. Or maybe it's because I saw sorrow in his eyes whenever we would talk and process life.

I remember once my cousin Carlos was clowning me and said, "That's why yo daddy a crack head!"

Of course, I didn't believe it, and it made me so mad. There was no way it could be true. Then years later when I found out it *was* true, it made me even sadder because I'd always been protective of my dad.

Teen Years with Daddy

When I was around eleven or twelve years old is when I really began to know my grandmother Alberta Moore, also known as Grandma Honey. She was from Mississippi and carried a lot of her southern ways and sayings to Cleveland where she raised her family with Granddaddy. I loved how she united the family with her dinners. Every holiday she cooked a big meal, and the only thing I hated were the chitterlings. Even though she was small in stature, she had no problem telling you about yourself for better or for worse. The last thing I wanted to do was upset her because once those gold teeth got to smacking, I knew I was only a couple words away from getting the switch. She was a stick of dynamite, but the firm woman who didn't play with kids became a dear grandmother to me as we spent time together.

We bonded as we grocery shopped and watched Cleveland Indians games. She would tell me I was special to her and that I would be something someday. I still hear her voice when I ride down Eighty-seventh street and see the empty field where her house once stood. Lord knows I hated the hours she made me till her garden, but I love what she was to me and how much she impacted my life.

I didn't know it as a child, but she was also the rock that held my father together. He lived with her on and off after he and my mom's divorce. My sophomore year of high school I got the call that my grandma died on the way to the hospital. I was in shock and worried about what it would mean for our family. My father fell into a deep depression that kept him from moving forward.

Daddy stayed at my Grandma's house with Granddaddy. We watched as he went to work, drank, and repeated the cycle. A few times he forgot my birthday. Other times he didn't buy us Christmas gifts. There were even times that he borrowed money from me for drinks. My eighth grade graduation was filled with tears because he wasn't there. I couldn't care less about awards and going to high school. I just wanted him back. Those times were a stark contrast to the earlier years. His broken promises caused me to realize I couldn't trust him anymore.

Breaking Point

One night as I was leaving work my dad called me. As the conversation progressed, I realized that he wasn't in a good place emotionally. My father was the type of guy who could laugh off pain and deflect, but this time he wasn't. As I heard him talk about life, I knew he was depressed. After a pause I said, "Daddy have you tried Jesus?" He was surprised by the question and asked me to tell him more about that.

For years I had been trying to encourage my dad with the love of God. I saw how much Jesus changed my life, and I knew he could be a comfort to my dad. I didn't have any promises of prosperity, or a quick fix to his problem, but I knew he didn't have anything left to lose and everything to gain. As I began to tell him about Jesus, my father seemed like he was listening but soon interjected and said he needed to call me back because he needed to go to the store. I knew what that meant. He was going to get a 40 ounce of malt liquor and drink away his sorrows. I waited for a few hours for him to call back that night, but he didn't.

The next morning, I woke up to a phone call from my dad, and he was sober. He asked me to continue telling him what I had begun talking about the night before. I quickly prayed and began to share my faith with him. After talking I asked him if he wanted to meet Jesus for himself. I was nervous as I asked him because I had prayed for this moment for a long time. What he shrugged off for years fell like fresh snow in December. That day my father asked Jesus to become the Lord of his life.

The months to follow were hard as I didn't see any fruit of my dad's newfound faith. In my immaturity I hoped my father would change immediately. I neglected to remember the years of chiseling I went through. A year later we talked on the phone, and my father seemed like he was in a dark place again. He knew Jesus, but the depression seemed thicker than before. After we finished our conversation, I felt like God was showing me that my father needed a new environment for a season. Around that time I'd began to develop a relationship with Craig Vincent who ran the men's shelter at the City Mission in Cleveland. I had asked him if he would be willing to take my father in, and he agreed if my father would be willing to come. I was nervous to bring it up to my dad. I was afraid he would be insulted by my request because he had a home. But I just knew the rehab and faith components would be life altering for him if he accepted the offer. The mission treated the men with respect and dignity, unlike many other shelters. I asked my father if he would be willing to leave everything he knew behind and try something drastic. I asked him if he would come live in the men's shelter. That week my dad packed a small bag and went to the City Mission.

The first couple of months new men were given a mattress downstairs as they waited for a bed to open up in the upper levels. This was also a period that showed which men were really willing to forsake everything to be better. If they made it past the early months, they joined a rigorous Bible-based program that led to a graduation and new growth. My father entered the mission as a man searching and left as a man with newfound faith and vision. I was so proud of him.

After graduating my Dad got his own place in downtown Cleveland. He wasn't on drugs, his drinking dwindled down drastically, and he began to attend church regularly. When we looked at each other at my college graduation and wedding ceremonies I knew that I was one of his dreams that came true and he was one of mine. For a person who experiences so much sorrow and pain I was proud to be able to make him proud.

On March 11, 2015, my father passed way after a six-month battle with stomach cancer. His funeral was packed with people from different walks of life. Their stories were a testament to how many people he blessed with his presence. Story after story gave me more of an appreciation for the man that he was. Many times in life we don't get to see the fruit of our hours of praying and hoping. This wasn't one of those times. It took years, but It was well worth the wait. The man who would ask me to borrow money to feed his addictions became one of the people who gave more to me than anyone ever could. He inspired me to be better, to believe deeper in the God who transformed his life.

My daddy wasn't perfect, but he was perfect for me.

Chapter 7 | Finding My Stride

As you move closer to your dreams and becoming the person God made you to be, things change. Your friends change. Your ideas about romance changes. The way you manage money changes. Your faith changes. Everything changes.

In fall 2017 my wife and I experienced these changes like never before. We were coming off a summer where we lost three of my former teens to gun violence. She had accepted a full-time position as a therapist in a Chicago neighborhood with the hopes of de-stigmatizing mental health. We had moved from our apartment of five years to a new one. The church plant where we served shut its doors. I had left my job as a youth minister to pursue music and speaking full time, which cut my earnings down to a third of what I had been making. The last thing I had were my close friendships, and even those changed. I soon found out that even my faith and music would change as well.

Permission Evangelism

During my early days in Chicago I attended Christ Bible Church on the South Side. While I was there, I heard Pastor James Ford share many stories that impacted me deeply as a Christian man. One evening he began to share about a woman who had attended their church for many years. She was devout in her service to God and the ministry. She attended various activities and services and volunteered when needed. Often she would ask her husband to attend with her. He was not a regular to say the least and had no interest in being there. She had tried for years to get him to go, but he was not having it.

One Sunday she was challenged to be available in the coming week to someone she cared about who didn't know Jesus. Her task was to simply be in their space and allow them to dictate the terms (without sinning of course). Well, one night that week as her husband began to put on his jacket to go to the pool hall, he was shocked to see her putting on her coat to come with him. She had never had time to go with him because of her vigorous church schedule.

They had a great time together, and without being prompted he returned the gesture on Sunday morning. She was blown away and excited that her love was finally attending church with her after all those years. When they got there not only did he enjoy the service, but he met the Lord and never stopped attending.

I loved this story because it reminded me that I need to be with people where they are—without judgement or agenda, I just needed to be present. This was the first of my shift in faith values.

Recovering Fourth Member of the Trinity

A well-known speaker and Chicago advocate Amy Williams always says that she is a recovering fourth member of the Trinity. It always gets a chuckle or two, but these days I'm living in that reality. I'm learning how to rest in the knowledge that God is at work even when I'm not.

In all honesty I'm not always in that frame of mind. I've heard countless pastors talk about the art of trusting God to work while we rest. I've reminded groups who come to serve in the hood that God was here and working before they arrived. I've seen God do special things in people's lives with a loose word I gave or small seed I've planted. But I still struggle with the reality of Him not needing my help.

The story about the woman who met her husband where he was in the pool hall, redirected my misguided thoughts about God needing to have me working for Him. It forced me to ask some real questions that I wasn't ready to answer. Do I really trust that the Holy Spirit is moving even when I'm not? Do I believe the seeds I've planted are enough? Am I willing to wait even if I never see the fruit of my labor? Am I having honest conversations that don't force others in a corner? Am I willing to sacrifice my feelings of having "victorious conversion moments" and just love people where they are?

When I wrestled with these questions it changed my whole philosophy of how I shared my faith. It made me redirect the way I wrote music. It rocked the core of what I thought it meant to be a Christian man. Like many evangelical Christians in America I suffered from the negative effects of Billy Graham culture. I believe that Dr. Bill Graham did some amazing things to set the table for faith to flourish all over the world, but because of his successful work, many of us have adopted the model of quick revival.

It's hard for Christian workers to admit they spent fifteen years with a group of people and only have one convert to show for it. That won't get you invited to do Christian TED talks. Instead we would rather set up a stadium and see millions meet Jesus. Now that's a resume builder. I'm not saying there isn't room for events, and large gatherings of faith, but what I'm saying is that our culture has leaned on them so much that it even affects our everyday interactions with people.

As a child I remember watching my grandfather make popcorn. He never used microwave popcorn bags. He would butter the bottom of a large pot and add the popcorn kernels. Then he would put the lid on the pot. Five or ten minutes later we would hear a kernel hit the side of the pot. It seemed to take forever, but then we'd hear another and another and before we knew it, we'd have a beautiful pot full of popcorn.

For years I lived my Christian faith opposite of my grandfather's popcorn. I wanted microwave popcorn. I wanted people to know the amazing God I knew at the moment we met. I wanted my music career to take off the moment I started. I wanted to take my growth to the next level without conquering my present devils. I didn't want the slow cooked popcorn. I wanted the fast stuff.

I later found out microwaved popcorn uses a chemical called perfluorooctanoic (PFOA). PFOA has been linked to cancers and hormone changes. In other words, the fast easy stuff may top me off, but if I embrace it long enough it will kill me!

So I stopped trying to make things happen fast. I stopped being a fourth member of the Trinity. I just embraced being a man after God's own heart who happens to make music. I made music without the agenda of saving people. I lived life without the flux of being people's savior. At first it was the hardest thing I'd ever done. All I knew was aggressive evangelical ministry, but for the first time ever I had to confront my own mortality and ask who I am apart from "doing Christian stuff." Do I matter if I'm not moving toward being prolific in all things Christian? Is God displeased with me because I'm not someone's pastor? Am I okay even if I'm missing a once-in-a-lifetime opportunity while I'm finding myself?

Struggles Being Evangelical

> Good thing my faith doesn't live or die on the back of evangelicalism because boy is it trippin! Every other hashtag is about peoples hurt or disgust with the American evangelical church. I promise that Jesus is so much better than what's being telecasted.

These were the words I posted on Facebook after reading numerous comments about people having church hurt following the #MeToo stories,

Black Lives Matters struggles, and the tensions of President Trump's election. My heart was torn by the actions, and even more so by the responses of my brothers and sisters of the white evangelical church. Sixty-five people liked my post, and a few commented with "Amen", "Yes Sir", and "Preach." I'm rarely one to vent on social media but for some reason I just had to that day.

One brother whom I deeply respect and love quoted F. F. Bruce: "To believe in the God who justifies the ungodly is to be evangelical."

He continued by sharing that he struggled with me using the word evangelical in a negative light. I actually agreed with him to that end and admitted I should have articulated better. I wasn't against being an evangelical. I was against evangelicalism, which held different connotations in 2018 than it did thirty years prior when Dr. Bruce wrote his words.

The journey to this Facebook post began with my ministry work in Chicago. I was hit with a fire hose of justice-oriented gospel teachings. I had read the whole Bible, studied it every day at Bible college, served in various ministries, and had been a Christian for ten years at that point. But my time on the Southside shook me the most because I comprehended God's heart for the city and what that meant for people like me. The kid who grew up in Cleveland and wondered why he didn't always feel at home in evangelical church circles. Of course, my church leaders back home made me feel like I mattered. They taught great gospel truths, but I don't think I ever comprehended the city around me and how she ached with pains of physical, spiritual, and social injustice.

One day I was at praise team practice and a church member came in and asked if anyone had a jimmy to help her get into her car because she locked herself out. The lady next to me gave me a loving nudge and smiled while whispering, "I bet you know how to get in it." I was a little confused at first and then disappointed as I realized I was the only person of color in the room. That's always been reality for me as a black Christian.

I've always lived in two different spaces. One where I saw gang violence, drug dealing, and the woes of the hood—black folk problems. Then the other that consisted of two parent homes, plush conferences, and amazing scenic trips—church life. I had to be the same person in both places and balance my Christian call to make disciples for God's kingdom. I became an evangelical hybrid, and I navigated it with ease throughout my late teens and early twenties.

Ferguson Hit Home

In 2014 the nation was in an uproar over the police shooting of unarmed teen Mike Brown. This was nothing new to me, so at first I just did like I do with most shootings I hear about—I compartmentalized it. I placed that traumatic experience in my "that's just how it goes" folder with all my others. I had lost a few teens to gun violence at that point. I knew the game, so I wasn't too shocked or angry. But for some reason compartmentalizing it wasn't enough for my coworkers at Young Life. A few asked me how I was feeling, and I assured them I was fine. Then one of them asked me to host a small group at our ministry and share my perspective on the issue. I really didn't have one. I knew there had always been tension with black people and cops. I knew we would always be seen as a group of people the country had to deal with like that family member you have to invite to the family reunion, no one really wants them there, but you can't not invite them. So, I have no idea why I agreed to do it.

Like any lesson I taught I didn't want to wing it, so I began to do some research and listen to interviews to see what was going on and why it blew up the way it did. As I listened and learned something was awakened and I realized that my internalized understanding of life as a black man in America was not normal. I always instinctively knew being black in America was different than being white, but now I emotionally knew it and owned it. I shared the lesson with my mostly white coworkers, and we just sat for a while. Some wanted immediate solutions, but we didn't have any. The answers we did have were just philosophical ideas that may never see the light of day.

As I began sharing that lesson with different groups, I would be very honest in saying that I really don't believe America's treatment of black or brown people would ever change and sadly nor did I believe it would change in the evangelical church. When conversations of race are brought up on social media, huge arguments erupt. Conferences I attend always seem to have one token black person in a line up full of white men. The black speakers talk about diversity or urban ministry but rarely, if ever, about marriage, pastoral ministry, or missions.

One year I went to a few conferences and tuned out, not because what was being shared wasn't applicable or Christian enough but because I was tired of not seeing new minority leaders. I was frustrated that all the worship was the same. The booklets featured hipster fonts and possibly a white Jesus. None of the panels included the people their guests talked about serving.

There were countless white leaders who talked about leaving a legacy in the under resourced communities in which they served, but they never gave up the ministries and its resources to leaders that reflected its community. Behind closed doors I would hear the angst of frustrated minority leaders who were passed over for leadership opportunities. Surely the people with money would never give to a ministry led by a black person. I guess the conferences just caught my cup when it overflowed, and it all just sickened me.

All these catalysts drastically changed the way that I viewed American Christianity and my place in it. I'll never be the same again, and I believe it's for the better.

Chapter 8 | I'm a Real American

After finishing a long day of speaking in Columbus, I got a call from an old friend, Tim Richards. I hadn't heard from Tim in years, but his number still popped up on my caller ID. Tim was the camp director of a camp where the Bruthahood and I rapped at in my early twenties.

When I picked up Tim began to tell me about a trip he was helping facilitate to Poland. Somehow he had a friend who hosted musical tours through Poland, and he thought of me as a potential artist. I had never been out of the country (other than Canada), so the opportunity thoroughly excited me. When I returned to Chicago, the tour director, Richard Dietrich, flew in to meet my wife and me as he wanted to make sure we were serious about our faith and share his Poland tour story in person.

How this Trip Began

Richard went on a mission's trip to Poland with the hopes of performing with Kirk Franklin. When he got there his vision was shattered as he realized Kirk didn't need him. He was crushed but determined not to let the trip go to waste. He proceeded to get his wife a special gift to bring back home. Her family was from a small village in Poland, so he decided to go there and get a copy of her family tree.

He had directions on a napkin to aid him in his journey, but he soon found himself lost. Unable to read the Polish street signs, he went into a gas station to ask for help, but no one spoke English. He was in big trouble and the anxiety began to build. Another driver pulled into the gas station, and to his surprise he spoke English. The man not only knew where he was going but drove him to the village. Richard told me he wouldn't be shocked if the guy was an angel in disguise.

When he got to the town hall, he asked for a copy of the family records for the Von Promonitz family. Suddenly the attendant paused and then got up to go to another room. When she returned, she said that he had to see the mayor. When he arrived at the mayor's office, he didn't know what to think. Was he in trouble or something? The mayor proceeded to express his deepest apologies for recently selling his family's castle.

As the conversation continued Richard was amazed to find out that his wife was a part of the royal family that the country thought had died. When the country was under attack, they fled and ended up in America. Turns out they owned four castles and over thirty mansions around the country. Their family crest was in schools and churches all over the area. God had just opened a door that Richard never imagined. I think it's safe to say that this new opportunity was way better than going on tour as a backup guitarist.

Goals

This story was too crazy to be true! I had some unexpected God moments in my life, but this one took the cake. A camp director who heard me rap more than ten years prior (when I wasn't that good) calls me out of the blue not even sure if I still rapped and invites me to Poland. Then the leader of the tour meets me the next night and shares a Princess Diaries story with pictures to back it up. I had to look around the dinner booth to find the cameras because surely I was getting punk'd by someone.

After doing more research and talking with my wife, we were sure this was legit. I was presented the opportunity to join the tour, and I quickly said yes. The only obstacle was that I would need to raise three thousand dollars. The ministry I was partnering with to attend was a short-term missions agency so they didn't fund the trip cost of touring bands. Richard's family wanted to maintain a healthy relationship with the Polish people, so they chose not to take all their land and castles from the state. This still allowed them total access and relationships with Polish officials that others would die for. From its inception this tour functioned as an experience with American Christian music for the Polish people.

I didn't want to go alone as Richard told me the events would be too big and strenuous to not bring a band. So I reached out to several friends and after a few weeks into the fund-raising all but my ride-or-die Liv Roskos backed out. We still needed a DJ, so we enlisted our friend Ron. Ron was a master turntablist and had recently left his job to pursue DJing full-time. Since he lived off his performances, he couldn't afford to pay for a trip of that magnitude, so I decided to raise his funds too. I committed to raising six thousand dollars total!

One more detail I forgot to mention—I was still raising my salary from my recent shift from Sunshine to full-time music. Me raising money added gray hairs to my wife's crown. She had been on this road before and watched God provide at the very last minute in unconventional ways, but this time she began preparing to console me once I missed the goal. This was a whole new level. Six grand in three months while also raising our livelihood. Jesus take the wheel!

We threw fundraiser concerts, made hundreds of calls, and sent up lots of prayers. Our team goal was literally met two days before our trip.

When In Poland

Four thousand people crowded in the town square as we began our headlining set at the Daisy Days Festival. Two days prior we were the opening act but the response to our music was so strong the team decided to place us last at every tour stop. We played in bars that were older than America and ran into some of the friendliest people I've ever met.

One couple we met was in their early twenties and began making out in the corner of the bar as we played. I figured they were some young teens just necking, but after we met them, I found out they were married and had three children. They got to get a night out, so they let the romance fly. They were also Christians. They and their children met us again three days later when we did a show in Germany.

The second day we were doing music at a high school and four days later a group of teens from the high school met us at another concert. They even rapped along. They had memorized the lyrics from just days before. We kept meeting folks with beautiful stories. After just about every show someone would offer to buy us a drink, so I became very familiar with the amazing wheat nectar of the

Polish. We talked with people about my music, faith, Poland, and American politics.

While we were in a couple of the bigger towns, I was shocked to see flyers promoting gospel concerts and singers in the public square. Our translator Aga told me that the Polish people loved to bring in black gospel artist because they identify with their struggle. Before Communism fell the Polish people were not allowed to listen to music freely, but when the regime fell in the 90s, they were flooded with the sounds of the 70s, 80s, and 90s. They loved music and really loved black gospel music because of its message about withstanding the weight of oppression. They had been oppressed and could identify.

The last thing I realized in Poland was probably the most profound of my journey. I am a real American. I know that sounds silly, but for years I had instinctively known that our country tolerates me but doesn't embrace me as her own. Real Americans cheer for the Dallas Cowboys, they listen to country music, they love steak, and are white. But I'm a Browns fan, I breathe Hip-Hop, I'm a pescatarian, and I'm black. In my neighborhood you rarely see flags on front porches, lawns, or in church sanctuaries. We don't say Happy Independence Day because our ancestors were slaves when the celebrations began. You might hear someone say, "Where we are cooking for the Fourth" but rarely "Happy Independence Day." We're not anti-American we just realize that we've never been American enough for America.

In Poland I wasn't a black man (though that was obvious). I was an American. They wanted to know my opinions on Donald Trump, Obama, and the current political climate. I've never been one to say I wish we were color blind; I actually can't stand that phrase. God loves our color and culture. To many being color blind means ignoring the past and its trauma, which is still raw and painful to me and to many. Being color blind means don't be black but conform to white American culture. This was a rare occasion when my color wasn't a barrier. I was the darkest one in the room and still very American.

The funny thing is, my Hip-Hop culture is actually one of the most American things you can find. It was bred out of struggle and oppression in America's urban centers. Even the collard greens I love to eat were the leftover plants the slave masters didn't want. The nasty pig intestines my ancestors made into chitterlings were necessary for their survival. God allowed a culture that became popular culture to rise from oppressed blacks in America.

I've heard people say if black people are so upset why don't they just leave our country, as if we would know where to go or want to leave our homes. On Twitter I read a Boston reporter say he witnessed a crowd chant "We hate Muslims we hate blacks give us our great country back" as President Trump claimed the Oval Office. The problem isn't with us not being American enough, we just won't stop until the values of our homeland are upheld. As American as I am it took me leaving the country to really realize it.

I keep a soft flex but I wanna keep it meek tho
These internet thugs on the boards wanna test me tho
Politics and torches got em feeling like a G
Wanna hang Kaepernick because the homie took a knee
I don't get it but I get it
All these Patriots so deflated
Pro-life is celebrated when its black its complicated
New level same Devil, new name same tweet
And we all think a post the same as getting in the street
Guess I'm sick of people pump faking with they purgery
Say you love God but keep yo money safely tucked away
The hood study drifting study drifting like a cast away

Soft Flex | CW Allen Album

Chapter 9 | The Marathon Continues

There Is Power in Being the Guest

They came to Bethsaida, and some people brought a blind man and begged Jesus to touch him. He took the blind man by the hand and led him outside the village. When he had spit on the man's eyes and put his hands on him, Jesus asked, "Do you see anything?" He looked up and said, "I see people; they look like trees walking around." Once more Jesus put his hands on the man's eyes. Then his eyes were opened, his sight was restored, and he saw everything clearly. Jesus sent him home, saying, "Don't even go into the village." (Mark 8:22-26)

If you did a deep dive into this Bible story you would see lots of the cultural and historical norms being broken by Jesus. Some folks would notice that people brought the man to Jesus showing a need for others to introduce us to God. You would also gain a great understanding of how Jesus is willing to spend time and care for people when others might not. You may even see the undoubtable truth that Jesus was more than a man because he could heal at will.

But as I look at it, I'm struck by how Jesus adjusted this Man's sight. It's not until he touches the man a second time that he sees properly. At first the man sees people, and they looked like trees. In a non-literal way, I often see people like trees as well. Even though I have been touched by the God of the universe I am prone to stereotypes, gossip, and have my own presuppositions of others. I see others like trees instead of people created in the image of God. But this reality isn't a CW issue, it's a humanity issue.

One day a young man from a visiting missions group came to our neighborhood and eagerly asked the director of our BridgeBuilders program when they would be going out to evangelize in the neighborhood. The director looked at the participant and asked if they did a lot of evangelism back home. The young visitor seemed to be puzzled by the question. He told the director he never goes out to evangelize back home. She asked him then why did he feel the need to do it in our neighborhood. I believe he felt the need to because the people in our neighborhood looked like trees to him.

Like this director, the founders of Sunshine Gospel Ministries' BridgeBuilders program wrestled with similar questions as groups sought to visit our "bad" neighborhood and make it Christian. They brought an extra measure of energy and enthusiasm that our staff appreciated, but they also tended to bring a theology that taught that they were bringing Jesus to our under-resourced neighborhood. This bred what many call a savior mentality. They would even pay to help us host them, but they never received anything back. It was the same story with suburban church partners. As the staff thought deeply about this transactional way of ministry they realized it's not a reciprocal friendship if only one person pays for dinner every meal. Nor is it a meaningful relationship when the person receiving the free meal never gets an opportunity to challenge or speak into the friendship. As a result, BridgeBuilders, a mission's trip with a twist, was born. Groups would come to our ministry and serve, but even more so they would learn.

As you have probably noticed from my earlier chapters I struggle with ministry and short-term missions' trips that stroke the egos of its participants. When short-term work allows the privileged to be the hero in its narrative, there's a problem. They get to post a great picture and quote with the people they just "saved." How much more powerful is it when those who thought they were coming to serve end up being taught and challenged by our neighbors. How beautiful the narrative that says those who have less financially, have rich amounts of faith, experiences, and culture to share. I love the dynamic of this programming.

It reminds me of John 4:

> Now Jesus learned that the Pharisees had heard that he was gaining and baptizing more disciples than John—although in fact it was not Jesus who baptized, but his disciples. So he left Judea and went back once more to Galilee. Now he had to go through Samaria. So he came to a town in Samaria called Sychar, near the plot of ground Jacob had given to his son Joseph. Jacob's well was there, and Jesus, tired as he was from the journey, sat down by the well. It was about noon. When a Samaritan woman came to draw water, Jesus said to her, *"Will you give me a drink?"* (His disciples had gone into the town to buy food.)
>
> The Samaritan woman said to him, *"You are a Jew and I am a Samaritan woman. How can you ask*

me for a drink?" (For Jews do not associate with Samaritans.)

Jesus answered her, *"If you knew the gift of God and who it is that asks you for a drink, you would have asked him and he would have given you living water."*

"Sir," the woman said, "you have nothing to draw with and the well is deep. Where can you get this living water? Are you greater than our father Jacob, who gave us the well and drank from it himself, as did also his sons and his livestock?"

Jesus answered, *"Everyone who drinks this water will be thirsty again, 14 but whoever drinks the water I give them will never thirst. Indeed, the water I give them will become in them a spring of water welling up to eternal life."*

The woman said to him, "Sir, give me this water so that I won't get thirsty and have to keep coming here to draw water."

He told her, *"Go, call your husband and come back."*

"I have no husband," she replied.

Jesus said to her, *"You are right when you say you have no husband. The fact is, you have had five husbands, and the man you now have is not your husband. What you have just said is quite true."*

"Sir," the woman said, "I can see that you are a prophet. Our ancestors worshiped on this mountain, but you Jews claim that the place where we must worship is in Jerusalem."

"Woman," Jesus replied, *"believe me, a time is coming when you will worship the Father neither on this mountain nor in Jerusalem. You Samaritans worship what you do not know; we worship what we do know, for salvation is from the Jews. Yet a time is coming and has now come when the true worshipers will worship the Father in the Spirit and in truth, for they are the kind of worshipers the Father seeks. God is spirit, and his worshipers must worship in the Spirit and in truth."*

The woman said, "I know that Messiah" (called Christ) "is coming. When he comes, he will explain everything to us."

Then Jesus declared, *"I, the one speaking to you— I am he."* (John 4:1-26)

For your sake I won't geek out on you with all the biblical insights of this text, but there are some things we must see as we jump into this story.

"I, the one speaking to you—I am he."

(John 4:1-26)

One, Jesus was Jewish. The Jews avoided Samaritans at all cost. Samaritans were only half Jewish, and in that day that was a huge disgrace. They also reminded the Jews of a time when they were oppressed by the people their ancestors co-mingled with to make the Samaritans. The Samaritans worshipped a different God on their mountain. Jews were to worship the true and living God and only in Jerusalem. Because of all these things Jewish folks avoided Samaria and Sychar at all cost. A Jewish person would add days to their journey just to walk around Samaria rather than travel through it.

Two, Jesus was a man. Jewish men didn't talk to women in public especially one on one! The author made a note that his disciples left, but when they returned, they were shocked to see Jesus associating with her.

Three, the woman was at the well alone. Most scholars believe that this woman was either a prostitute or carried a lot of shame in her community because she had five husbands and the one she was with now wasn't her husband. That's another strike in that culture. She was getting water at noon. Nobody did that. Noon is the hottest part of the day and in a desert climate that's a death wish. It's safe to say that she didn't want unwanted attention because she chose to attend the well at that time.

Four, Jesus became her guest. Jesus was such a captivating person because he always displays great intentionality. Notice how He broke all the norms (without sinning) just to meet this woman and ask her for a drink. His willingness to be the guest opened the door for her to be vulnerable with Him. Ultimately His willingness to be the guest, led to her and her whole village (that was ashamed of her) to encounter God.

There is power in being the guest. There is power in not being the host who dictates the terms. I love going to restaurants of different people groups who don't expect to see a black man patronize their business. What an honor to show them I value their food and culture. I may mess up the pronunciation of their dish, but the fact that I am willing to step into their world and enjoy it their way is a special thing. Have you ever been in an office and seen someone struggling to speak English and then someone comes from the backroom to fluently speak their language? Their whole posture changes. They become more expressive and may even crack a smile. There is power in being the guest!

I Am a BridgeBuilder

When I left Sunshine, I knew my time was up in youth ministry. The idea of chasing my teens around for camp permission forms and listening to the same cycle of ninth grade jokes just didn't help me get out of bed in the morning. As I pursued my music and speaking career, the BridgeBuilders (BB) program leaders would regularly invite me to continue speaking to groups who would visit the ministry. Eventually the director asked me to join him as a worker ten hours a week. I wasn't opposed to that commitment since I had already spent so much time doing the work of BridgeBuilders.

The months to follow were extremely rich and revitalizing. Tim Baldwin, the director, was a very welcoming man who had a doctorate in education and studied hospitality deeply. He had also spent years teaching and working in refugee resettlement work. It was obvious that his experiences being a guest of different cultures uniquely wired him for the work of BridgeBuilders. I loved hearing his perspective and seeing his teachable nature in our black context. He was what we call a "woke white boy."

Tim and I also developed a great working relationship even though we couldn't have been more different. I am black; he is white. He was in his fifties, and I was twenty years younger. I was welcoming my first daughter into the world, and he was welcoming a new grandchild. My language was Hip-Hop and storytelling; his was the rigor of academia. But one thing bonded us: Jesus. We both loved theology and seeing people treated justly. We also both loved to learn and teach. We only knew each other for a few months but it seemed like we had been friends for years.

One afternoon while we were sitting at a local jerk chicken restaurant Tim informed me he was moving to Chattanooga, Tennessee. He and his wife were looking to be closer to his son and grandchildren. Having medical challenges also began to take its toll on Tim as the BridgeBuilder program required twelve- and fifteen-hour days in the busy season. His departing only made sense. I was happy and also sad to see him leave.

After sharing he was about to leave, he asked if I would be interested in taking the role as the BB director. I was honored that he would think of me as a potential leader for such an important ministry. I loved the idea, but I wondered if I was the right guy to lead the program. Like every ministry, Sunshine has its issues. Some were misplaced assumptions by community members and others are legit critiques. I also wondered if senior staff members might still see me as the twenty-two-year-old CW who first came to Sunshine without knowing I had grown up immensely in that decade.

As I pondered the new possibility with my wife and close mentors, I was urged to talk to our executive director, Joel, and let him know what I was thinking. As I shared with Joel that I would be interested in becoming the director, I couldn't fully get a read if he wanted me or not. During the months of waiting and processing my future for the next few years, I was certain of a few things. Having black leadership could benefit BB as the make-up of our neighborhood and its subject matter spoke to the woes of black culture. It would be ideal for the next leader to live in and love the Southside. They should also be able to handle God's Word while interacting with different groups of people. The more I thought about it, the more I realized I was built for the job.

BridgeBuilders called for me to live out my culture through its curriculum. The program also had a strong emphasis on community building. Youth ministry allowed me to be creative in my planning but only to a certain degree. BridgeBuilders, on the other hand, called for me to use all my gifts and entrepreneurial leanings. When I was officially invited to become the new director, I walked in with confidence.

Nipsey Hussle

On March 31, 2019, I scrolled through my twitter feed to see hundreds of tweets saying R.I.P. to South LA Hip-Hop star Nipsey Hussle. As I read reports and listened to interviews about his murder, I was grieved. I didn't know him personally. I was simply a fan and a student of his music business moves, yet his death knocked the wind out of me. Also, my baby cousin was murdered a week prior, so l know I was still carrying that. I think a big part of my grief was that I saw myself and many other young black men doing community work living vicariously through Nipsey.

Not only was Nipsey recently nominated for his first Grammy, he had partnered with a tech mogul to create a co-working tech space in his community so that his neighbors could have access to the latest tech advances. His clothing store, The Marathon, provided basic items and jobs for community members, and he was still in the process of opening a barbershop, seafood restaurant, and youth basketball programs.

I was grateful to watch one of Crenshaw's gang members become such a transformative example for millions of people. I have no idea what he believed in, but I know he was a BridgeBuilder and community developer. He is what every Christian community ministry leader hopes is the outcome from their work. It was heart-wrenching to see the same community in which Nipsey grew up and invested in become the same one in which he was murdered. I pray that God would continue to raise up leaders in marginalized communities. Leaders who don't try to get out but ones who understand the value of investing in it.

The Marathon Continues

Chapter 10 | The Weight of a Father

My wife is the most important person in my life. She is my partner and best friend, except in the morning. Yep you heard me right, except in the morning. My wife loves to experience the sunrise and waking up to her jam-packed day. I am the exact opposite. I have no desire to communicate with anyone in the early hours of the day nor see the sunrise. So naturally I was not amused when Jacqueline woke me up on a Saturday morning God made for sleeping in.

"Dub, Dub, get up! When was my last period?"

"I don't know. Can we talk about it in an hour?"

"No, Dub, I missed my time of the month."

"Maybe your body changed your period time to match one of the ladies in the building. You know ya'll all sync up like the iPhone."

"Stop playing! I think I'm pregnant! I took two tests, and they both said positive."

When I heard the "P" word my eyes opened, and I rose like an extra in Michael Jackson's *Thriller*. Sure enough, my wife of seven years was pregnant. My mind raced with daydreams of our child. I surely would name him after my dad and me. Of course, he would be indoctrinated to be a steadfast Cleveland sports fan. Lastly, I would guide him in the ways of Jesus. I couldn't have asked for a more precious gift.

You Changed Everything

My wife and I waited patiently in the lobby of the 3-D gender reveal center. Our niece Mezzah

begged for every overpriced toy in the store while
the adults made wagers on the baby's gender.

I'm sitting in this gender reveal anticipating.

Knowing if I don't see blue that's devastating.

Then that light went pink, my heart got weak.

I'm about have a girl, I'm floored, can't speak.

- Everything | Catalyst

I was sure my wife was cooking little Dub in
her oven. Words could not describe how shocked
and disappointed I was when they announced we
were having a baby girl. I thought about how I
didn't know how to wipe a baby girl when it's time
to change her diaper. What if I say something that
hurts her feelings, and it steers her to the dark side?
My wife's tears are what really got me to thinking
as she articulated her fear in raising a young black
girl. "I don't know how to do her hair." (My wife

didn't grow up in a black community so it wasn't until her twenties that she learned where to go to properly treat her own black girl magic) How will the world treat her? Throughout history, the narrative of the black woman has never been favorable.

Fears of a Father

In 1810, English men and women gathered at a Piccadilly building in London to see various oddities and freaks of nature. As people entered, they crowded around a cage featuring a half-naked, young black woman named Sara Baartman. Four years after gaining immense popularity, Baartman was sold to a man who specialized in showcasing animals.

She traveled to Paris and was showcased as an animal for crowds of spectators. This gained even more attention and attracted the attention of anatomists, zoologists, and physiologists who studied her in attempts to link humans and animal species. A year following those experiments, she died at the young age of twenty-six. Her owner then dissected her body and displayed her body parts at the Musée de l'Homme (Museum of Man) until 1974. It wasn't until 2002 that her body was released for a proper burial in her native land of South Africa. Black women have been the object of the world's pleasure and abuse for centuries, and it continues to this day.

While searching for a home, my wife and I met a property owner name Ms. Sheila. She began to tell us amazing stories about her life, and we marveled at all she had accomplished. The house she was selling was just one of her properties. She was a self-made millionaire who made her fortune flipping houses before the housing market crash. I was struck by her resilience. Five years prior she had been diagnosed with cancer.

Ms. Sheila went into the doctor because she was having pains in her chest. They assured her she was fine, so she left the office believing it was only a bruise. A few weeks later the pain intensified, and she decided to get a second opinion. The second doctor said the same thing. It wasn't until her third complaint and her insisting on getting an X-ray that they found out she had stage three breast cancer. By God's grace she changed her lifestyle and won her battle with cancer.

Ms. Sheila is not alone in her story about the healthcare system's treatment of black women. Many books have been published that address this sad truth, but this is no new reality to black women. There is a myth that black people are stronger than other races and therefore they aren't taken seriously unless they over-exaggerate their medical woes. In most cases black women are ignored and told they will be ok until it's too late.

This past year my wife and I watched the *Surviving R. Kelly* docuseries. For me the show really hit home because R. Kelly was my favorite R&B artist. (I know a number of his albums word for word.) In the docuseries countless mothers and entertainment specialists shared their stories surrounding the artist's brainwashing and abducting of underage black girls. In a huge way I felt complicit in letting this happen because like most of the world, we knew, we were warned, but we didn't care.

We packed out his shows, stepped in the name of love at our weddings, and enabled his behavior at the expense of young black women. When asked how the world could let this happen, the response across the board was that we just didn't care because they were black girls. If they were white we would have kicked down R. Kelly's doors. What a sad commentary on our society. The narrative has not changed much, if at all, since Sara Baartman.

According to the National Center for Education Statistics, in the academic year of 2015-16, black women were the most educated people group in the country with 64 percent earning bachelor's degrees. The country villainized black men in the late 80s, so black woman became the glue that held our communities together. Throughout the decades, black women in America have been groundbreaking pioneers who invented, taught, and set trends that the rest of the world can only re-fabricate.

I am so thankful for the amazing women that God has allowed to shape my life. The grandmother who helped raise me just turned 102. She also mothered eight successful children. My mother has always been a respectable, classy lady. Not only is she beautiful on the outside, but she is stunning on the inside. She raised four kids as a single woman most of our childhoods. I never heard her talk negatively about my father even when he was struggling. When my father died, she helped me plan and pay for his funeral services. Some family members couldn't believe his ex-wife would do so much and not have an ulterior motive.

But, that's exactly who she was raised to be a caring compassionate woman.

I could name all the women in my life and list the amazing attributes they possess, but I'll just say that my daughter has a rich and vibrant lineage. Yet we were still wrestling with the reality of what this world will attempt to teach her about her worth. I feel the weight of knowing how important my job is as a father.

Ariah

On Saturday August 23, 2019 I was getting prepared to go rap at one of our community's elementary school pep rallies. God had other plans. Instead my wife's water broke, and we rushed to the hospital. The next morning, I watched Ariah, my princess, enter this world. That first night I held her, I talked to her, and most of all I prayed for her. As she looked up at me, I knew I had just been given the greatest gift a man could be given: a baby girl to love and protect.

Over the next couple of months, a revival began in my heart. I wanted to be closer to God. I wanted Ariah to know how important He was. The Lord used her to help me scratch the surface of understanding how much He loves His children.

> The Spirit you received does not make you slaves, so that you live in fear again; rather, the Spirit you received brought about your adoption to sonship. And by him we cry, "Abba, Father." (Romans 8:15)

> He predestined us for adoption to sonship through Jesus Christ, in accordance with his pleasure and will. (Ephesians 1:5)

> See what great love the Father has lavished on us, that we should be called children of God! And that is what we are! The reason the world

does not know us is that it did not know him.
(1 John 3:1)

Often in my relationship with God I have been more fearful of him taking away stuff or punishing me than focused on how much He likes and loves me! His love for me isn't accidental. He intentionally adopted me into His family, giving me the same rights as a natural born son. He loves me more than I love myself.

When I'm deathly tired from work and my baby cries, I get up to change and feed her. Her entry into this world hijacked my sex life, and I'm ok with that because she means more than my own desires. I love her but not as much as God loves us all.

I still can't believe I get to be ya daddy.
And even when I hurt ya feelings I hope ya checking for
me.
Already ya biggest fan, I'm down to confide
No pride, no pride, I kicked my cat to the side.

You so dignified it's like you from Wakanda.

High majesty so carry yourself with honor.

Never let the slick words distract God the Father.

And if them goons acting up, we got the shootie for ya.

You don changed everything. Baby, you my everything.

Tryin' to catch my breath I can't breathe.

Can't breathe.

You don changed everything. Baby, you my everything.

Girl, you know I'm never gon leave.

Gon leave.

I can't live without you and just heard about ya.

The best that I do, I can't live without ya yeah.

You don changed everything. Baby, you my everything.

Girl you know I'm never gon leave.

-Everything | The Dream Baby 2

Chapter 11 | The Dream Baby

Dreaming for a Reason

My mother would always take us to her AA meetings. Sometimes I loved it, but most times I hated it. The ones I loved were the ones with things for us kids to do as the attendees testified to their victories over alcohol. They had just simple things like a playground or basketball hoop so we wouldn't have to sit through the whole thing. One meeting had a small nursery with children's books. I was nowhere near an advanced reader as a child, but I was drawn to a white leather-bound book with gold letters. It was a Bible, but not just any

Bible. It was a children's Bible. It had pictures and everything.

I was a major comic book fan, so it interested me. I had always thought about God, but there had never been an intersecting point for us to hit it off. I couldn't understand all the thees and thous. God just seemed like a great idea for when I got older. For some reason that time felt different. I understood what I was reading, and it pained me to have to leave the book when we left the meeting. For hours I read the Old Testament stories, and one in particular really caught my attention. The story of a young boy named Joseph.

Joseph was the youngest of twelve brothers, and he was what my mama called "spoiled." The writer of the story says that Joseph was his father's favorite child, and he didn't hide it from the other children. They saw the amazing colorful coat he gave his son. They saw the attention and care he paid to Joseph, and it made them jealous. Along with his father's spoiling, Joseph seemed to be a jerk too.

God had given Joseph dreams of him becoming a ruler over his family, and he made sure his brothers knew every detail of how he would rule. In my neighborhood we would call that "sonning" someone. Sonning someone is the act of shaming them in front of others to make yourself look good. Joseph's brothers hated him for his audacity to *son* them, so they made a plan to get rid of him. As Joseph went to meet his brothers in the fields, they nearly beat him to death and sold him into slavery. The years to follow were the worst of his life.

He was falsely accused of attempting to rape an official's wife. He spent years in prison but somehow ended up the second in command of the world's most powerful empire at the time. God made the dream of an immature Joseph a reality! But before he could handle it with maturity, he had to be tried by the fire of life.

Years after I returned to Cleveland to visit, I had a newfound respect for my mother's AA meetings. She had been attending them for over twenty years and still faithfully served various newcomers around the city. On this particular occasion I went to hear her testify (share her story). I was blown away by how articulate and fun she was to listen to. She was a Joseph. God gave her both purpose and vision that would not have been possible without her years of mistakes and trials.

Since the first moment I read Joseph's story I felt a connection with him. I have not been sold into slavery, or given the ability interpret dreams. But what I am is a dreamer, and like Joseph after his trials, I am a man trying to use his gifts to better the community around me. Joseph's story compels me to ask what it would look like if the dreams we have are catalysts for God's larger purpose? What if the years of trials and learning who we are is just the training ground for God to use us in ways that we never imagined? Many people say they want to know God's will for their lives, and I want to take this last bit of our time together to share how we find our calling or God's will.

Knowing What You Are Called To

> Therefore, I urge you, brothers and sisters, in view of God's mercy, to offer your bodies as a living sacrifice, holy and pleasing to God—this is your true and proper worship. Do not conform to the pattern of this world but be transformed by the renewing of your mind. Then you will be able to test and approve what God's will is—his good, pleasing and perfect will. (Romans 12:1-3)

This is undoubtedly my favorite passage in the Bible. The Apostle Paul is writing to the Roman church, which was a very aggressive, fast-paced culture full of new and rebranded ideas. Rome was the powerhouse of the world and the place to be with four million people (60 percent of whom were slaves). They loved watching people fight in the Coliseum like UFC and applauded death like many horror movie watchers. The church was split between racial lines as the Gentile and Jewish house churches worshipped separately and didn't have any dealings with each other. Lastly, many people in Rome would probably say they were spiritual to some degree. Sound familiar?

In chapters 1-3 of Paul's letter to the Romans he outlines humanity's despite need for the gospel to be saved once and every single day. We all deserve to die for our sin. We all have the capacity to commit any sin in the book. We all are totally broken. Chapter 4 highlights Abraham while showing us that it is only by faith we can be saved from ourselves and the judgment we deserve. In chapters 5-8 we see the results of being right with God. Our rightness will broadcast the hope of God to a dying unbelieving world. Then in chapters 9-11 we are reminded that God will keep His promises to His people. When we arrive at chapter

12, Paul tells the Christians to not conform to the world but be renewed in their mind. He wanted them to test what God's will was.

In view of God's mercy or because of all that God has done, this is how you should respond. Paul is letting his listeners know that they are first called to know God. Notice that Paul says we are called to be a living sacrifice. All throughout the Bible we know that God's people had to kill the right animal and shed its blood to be forgiven for their sin. That sacrifice becomes dead and no longer of use, but Paul tells these Roman believers to be "living sacrifices." That means they are being called to dedicated to God over and over again. Their service and relationship with God never ends.

Next, Paul says that this is our "spiritual act of worship." The word *spiritual* used here is *logikos* in Greek. From the word *logikos* we get the word *logic,* which means rational or reasonable responses that are carefully thought through. If you really believe in Jesus' death, burial, and resurrection, if you really believe that He is the creator of everything, then our only logical and rational response is to be a living sacrifice.

The Greek word *klesis* used throughout the New Testament means "invitation" and is translated as *call* or *calling*. God invites us to meet Him and then be on assignment with Him. Often throughout the Bible we see the term *adoption* used, which is the most intimate invitation we see in Scripture. We are adopted into God's family. Being adopted into a family in biblical times was a huge deal.

I love the movie *Gladiator* with Russell Crow. In the beginning of the movie the dying Cesar shares his regrets with Maximus (Crow) and says he believes his son, who will soon become king, is not fit to be on the throne. He tells Maximus he wants to take him in as his own son and make him the next Caesar. This was not uncommon if a Caesar was displeased with his heir to the throne.

By adopting Maximus as his son no one would ever see him as an outsider of the family. Every right and claim to inheritance would be given to the adopted son. He even took the family name. In his letter to the Ephesians Paul wrote "adopted sons" because in that day only sons were entitled to inheritance. (It's messed up, but I've heard worse.) In reality God makes use of both males and females. Both can be adopted into his family.

Next we notice that we are called to know ourselves. I never realized this was a calling, but it is. Knowing yourself enables you to make the most of your time on earth in an undivided way.

I have a friend named Temeka, and she loved hanging out in coffee shops. Temeka's family and friends would tell her she was wasting too much time there, but she loved it. She could tell you all the different coffee beans and what is brewing just by the smell. Eventually Temeka started to think a little deeper about why she loved coffee shops so much and realized that she wanted to run one.

Soon after Temeka wrote a business plan and opened a coffee shop. Like Temeka we all have God given bents and should explore them.

Another way of knowing ourselves is to know our personality. Are you serious? Do you love to joke? Do you live by the spreadsheet, or do you live carefree? Your personality plays a big a part in what you like. If you've ever had a relationship that ended, it was because in some way your personalities probably clashed. Personalities are a great aid in helping us develop community and knowing where we shouldn't be. Our personality helps us know how to relax, plan, and be patient in our triggered moments.

As we continue diving, we find that talents are another great indicator as well. You may not have a lot of talents, but everyone has *some* type of talent. Your talents may very well inform your career, hobbies, or volunteering. You only need to watch one bad audition of American Idol to see that your humming friend probably has talent those contestants could only dream of.

When we meet Jesus, God continues to affirm our adoption when He gives us spiritual gifts. They aren't talents because talents can be self-serving and done without being a Christian. Spiritual gifts are only possessed by believers, and they are to be used in the building up of His church. Bible teaching, administration, helps, mercy, encouragement, exhortation, discernment, leadership, shepherding, prophecy, tongues—these are all spiritual gifts. They are validated by God, the Bible, and your Christian community. We all have a lane. Find yours.

The last part of knowing ourselves is knowing our sovereign history or our ordered history.

One day I had a brother at my house, and he was talking to me and Jac. He was half joking when he told me I wasn't black anymore. It triggered me in ways I can't explain. It's not that I resented folks who aren't black, but being an African American man is a part of my sovereign history. It's a part of who I am, and I take joy in my heritage. I hated the fact that he and many others equate my skin color to never talking properly, eating only certain foods, sagging, and fighting to solve my problems. I have experienced the tranquility and the stress of the hood. I've also experienced the beauty and brokenness of the burbs. They both informed my sovereign history.

Not all of our sovereign histories are fun, yet God has a way of using them all in the end. Every hurt we've felt, every skill we've learned, the places we've lived, and the way we came to know him, they all are a part of your ordered or allowed history.

Paul tells us not to be conformed to the "pattern of this world, but be transformed by the renewing of your mind" (Romans 12:2). To be conformed is to be shaped or molded by something or someone. The word *world* in this passage is best translated as temporary area, meaning a small part of a larger time period.

I was on Facebook and I saw a video from a former pastor talking about why Christianity isn't real and why he stopped following the white man's Jesus. He talked about how the Bible was copied from Egypt and Jesus was not God. He also said that the white man created our faith to enslave us. Of course, he was wrong, but the sad part is he represents millions of people who don't know their church history, which is a part of their sovereign history. Which in turn leads to a conformity to the patterns of this world.

It starts with missing church, not having real confession and spiritual tune ups with other believers, and then you're sinning without conscience. The next thing you know you're questioning everything you said you believe as you start fighting on the wrong side of sin. Don't get caught conforming! Remember "the grass withers, the flowers fall, but the word of God endures forever" (Isaiah 40:8). I can have a hit record, but no one will care ten or twenty years from now.

The only way not to conform is to renew our minds. How!? By reading God's Word, being with other believers, and being with God daily. The Holy Spirit living inside of us will do the rest. We also have to renew the way we see church. If we only see church as a place we go and not the people we are a part of, we forget its power. If it's only a place where we look nice and aren't honest when we have missed the mark, we are not really renewing our minds.

Knowing yourself affirms who you are in God. Your unique personality, talents, spiritual gifts, and sovereign history are a huge factor in knowing what God is calling you to. As we round third base and head home, the last thing we can learn from these Bible verses is that once we have internalized the first of our callings we are called to a unique assignment. Callings are for a season and can change with time. I may not rap forever. I will not always be a husband and father. As I write I am blind out of one of my eyes and writing books may not be a forever thing if my disease progresses. It's okay for things to change, but one thing remains: God will never leave us or forsake us. He invites us to know Him forever. He is the greatest catalyst we could ever encounter.

Thank Yous

Thank you to my Savior, Jesus Christ. You have been the biggest Catalyst of my life. In every journey, struggle, joy, and test, you have been there. I am grateful for our relationship, and I know you gave your very best to secure it. I am forever in your debt and I love it.

Thank you to my wife who pushes me to be better. You are the mother of my child, and for that gift I can never repay you. Your love has made me a better man, and I hope I can show you a fraction of the compassion you show me as I drive you crazy with my dreams. You are my everything.

To my family, I love you so much. We aren't perfect, but we are perfect for each other. You are a special part of my story that I will never neglect to appreciate. Mama you are my Shero. Your patience and loyalty to others is a sight to behold. Keith, I am grateful for the growth of our relationship over the years. You are a great man, and I believe in you. Thank you for loving my mother so much. I feel comfortable being in Chicago knowing you are there. Rob, Ashley, Tiffany, Dinky, and BooBop, I am honored to have you as siblings. Never let anyone (including yourself) tell you what you can't do.

Pastor Joe and Mama A, you are my other parents. I am blessed to be a part of your family. YFC Cleveland, SRBC, and the Bruthahood, you gave me a place to learn and find myself as a teen searching for meaning. Jonny and Liz Fine, Nat Harper, Kyro Taylor, Chris Withmore, Jeff Thompson, Mike Harper, Doug Roth, and Eloy Gonzales, you were the leaders who let me bounce around your homes for meals and events. You showed me a tangible example of people who love God and the world around them. I love you.

Sunshine Gospel Family past and present, you watched me become a man. You have cried with me, argued with me, and love my family like your own. My life changed the day you gave me an opportunity to join your lineage of world changers. My financial and prayer partners, you have given me encouragement when I've felt the loneliest. You keep giving and have a vision for my life and God's work through it. I have no words for my thankfulness towards you, so I'll just leave it at that.

Lastly, my fans, mentors, and peers, you will always be a part of this journey as well. Until the next time. I love you all.

About the Author

CW Allen was born and raised in Cleveland, Ohio, where he grew up listening to Hip-Hop music and fell in love with heart-pounding drum and bass lines. He began rapping his senior year of high school and never looked back. By that time he had already fallen deeply in love with God and His Word, so his music was just an expression of his heart and surroundings.

In 2009 CW left Cleveland and moved to Chicago where he attend Moody Bible Institute and studied communications and Bible. CW also met his lovely wife, Jacqueline, there. CW and Jacqueline welcomed their first child, Ariah Christine Allen, into this world in August 2019. They currently reside on Chicago's Southside where CW also works as the program director for Sunshine Gospel Ministries' BridgeBuilders program.

Now in the fifteenth year of his musical journey CW has finished his first book and latest album entitled *Catalyst*. CW has had the privilege to share all over the country in bars, schools, camps, and conferences opening for artists such as Cannon, Da Truth, Sean C. Johnson, Shopé, This'l, and the Legendary Curtis Blow.

CPSIA information can be obtained
at www.ICGtesting.com
Printed in the USA
FSHW020632290620

9 781734 638530